A Cry in the Night

The City of Lights' Dark Side

Mary S. Brown-Durr

outskirtspress
DENVER, COLORADO

Outskirts Press, Inc.
http://www.outskirtspress.com

ISBN: 978-1-4787-1227-5

Dedication

This book is dedicated to the brilliant and courageous people who were involved in the struggle for justice and equality for the Negro citizens of Canton, Mississippi. We, especially salute the many amazing people such as, Annie Gross, Ida Bennett, Julia Mae Small, Joseph Thompson, Ida V. Barnes, Johnny Goodloe, Lee Johnson, Ben Gross, Jessie J. Lacy, Margie B. Elder, William Milton, Theodore Hewitt, Eugene Patterson, Charlie Scott, Nelson Brown, Virgil Taylor, Mamie Jones, Barbara Brown, Susie Brown, Barney Smoot, Louis Jackson, Isadora Morgan, John E. Williams, Willie Ford, Charles Taylor, Ruben Greenwood, Ethel Carter, Frank Franklins, Frank Howard, Rev. Samuel Lee Anderson, Tommy Emory, Jr., Joseph Williams, Josie Lee McDonald, Robert Lee Walker, Mildred Williams, Bessie Harris, Gable Davis, Vietter Davis, Blanchie White, Mattie Williams, May Dell Thompson, C. O. Chinn, Sr., C. O. Chinn, Jr., George Raymond, Martha Jane Jones, J. A. Thomas, Jamie Travis, Mamie Small, Jessie Thomas, David Walker, John W. Thomas, Preston Cooper, Claretha Whisenton, Bodie P. Jones, Willie Harris, J. C. Horton, Clyde Goodson, Archie O. Ford, Rosie Ford, Archie Ford, Jr., Narcis Smith, Mack Smith, Tommie Lee Potts, Walter Small, Wash Luckett, George Day, A. C. Chambers, Deloris Brown, Clara Fleming, George Hewlett, Maxine Chambliss, Carry Anderson, James Anderson, Joe W. Fleming, Setha M. Anderson, Sylvia Grayson, Sylvia Hewitt, Percy Johnson, Isaac Chambers, James Anderson, Jr., Monroe Fields, Melvin Millsap, Melvin Douglas, Bowie James, Johnnie Owens, Berthie L. Meeks, Charlie David, Jr., Herald Henry Luckett, Edward Earl Ross, Arthur Thompson, Laura Smith, Leo Gross, Clarence McCullough, William L. Small, Benjamin L. Small, Alice L. Evans, Sallie Evans, W. J. Ware, Moses Drummond, Wilbert Robinson, Shirley Harris, Ortles Williams, Annette Hill, William Veal, William C. Jones, James Bennett, Johnnie Green, Matthew Green, Jessie Anderson, Phyllis Bailey, Doris

L. Hart, Lillian Jones, Robert Lee Griffin, Alice Collier, Ida Belle Horne, Leora Cain, Luanne Moore, Early Wright, Mary Mackie, Bessie M. Harris, Idonnia Jackson, Jonella Jackson, Leo Evans, Merry Ruston, Carrie Smoot, Elton Branson, Johnnie Bouldin, Robert Lee Bouldin, James E. Stokes, Marian Benjamin, Marshell Lee Blunt, Jessie J. Luckett, Robert Dykes, Floyd Bouldin, Charles Cooper, James Dozier, Jonathan Bailey, Clarence Anderson, Lawrence Jackson, Roosevelt Carter, Agnes Dotson, Walter Maberry, Sam Bouldin, Jr., Chester Williams, Willie Jones, Percy Anderson, Jr., Oscar Lee Smith, Willie E. Isadora, Tommie L. Spencer, Luther Mary Wilson, Maggie Marie Wilson, Sarah Wilson, Bill Banks, George Washington, Charlie Robinson, Edell Rodgers, Erma Mae Potts, Jessie Harris, MacArthur Cotton, Dave Dennis, James Farmer, Robert (Bod) Moses, and Joseph Rodgers for showing fearlessness in backing the Civil Rights Act of 1963-64, which pushed the passage of this legislation in its greatest form for all American citizens regardless of their race, creed, or national origin to become American citizens guaranteed by the United States Constitution.

It is also necessary to dedicate this book to Leroy Brown, Bessie Mae Hamlin, and Eddie Mixion, Jr.

To these magnificent people: Mr. Joe Brown and Mrs. Susie Mae Brown, the parents of Barbara Jean Brown, Ricky Brown, the son of Barbara Jean Brown, and the siblings' Bennie Fisher, Eliza Whitaker (deceased), Mary Sue Brown-Durr, Susie Mae Brown-Wilson, Carrie Mae Brown-Bennett, and my two friends—Gloria Williams and Rosie Thomas.

Table of Contents

Acknowledgments

In appreciation of all the remarkable people who took a stand against inequity, injustice, and racial hatred during those terrible times in the state of Mississippi, particularly, in Canton, Mississippi, there is a crown of glory for all of you.

Courtesy Of

The Mississippi Public Library of Archives and Records, Canton, Mississippi Public Library, and People Funeral Home of Canton, Mississippi.

Introduction

The murder of Barbara Jean Brown in the small town of Canton, Mississippi in Madison County, was an unforgettable event. The town, now the City of Lights, was once a town saturated with murder, hatred, violence, and darkness. The town's population was 26,000 Negros and 9,000 Whites. The town county seat was named after former President James Madison. Canton, Mississippi, was the embodiment of the traditional south during the Jim Crow era. It had immense boundaries of undeveloped lands once occupied by the Chickasaw Indians. Negros and whites arrived in Canton in search of the opportunity to make a living for their families.

The same ideology drew Joe Brown to Canton. He wanted the opportunity for a better life for his family, but did not know that when cotton prices plummeted, he would have to sell his land to pay off debts. He became a sharecropper.

The dominating white social body of Canton easily welcomed a new form of slavery by preventing Negros from the rights to vote by creating a $2 poll ballot tax, beyond the budget of most. Along with this restriction came racial segregation and lynching. The harrowing circumstances of Negros in Madison County continued to exist long after The Supreme Court challenge of 1988 in Williams v. the State of Mississippi (170, U.S.213, 1898). As well as the Mississippi State Legislatures' new Jim Crow law, House Bill 21 and House Bill 22. These bills, for example, House Bill 21 made it legal for all white businesses to refuse and provide services to all Negros. Additionally, granting white owned businesses sanction who post, *"management reserves the right to refuse to sell to, wait on, or serve any person"* from all penalties. Moreover, House Bill 22 made it illegal for Negros to use public facilities' drinking fountains, bathrooms, parks and recreation, businesses, etc., that are specifically not marked "COLOR ONLY." It quickly became apparent that the American Civil Rights Movement was disenchanted with the treatment of Negros as second class citizens and brought nationwide evidences to the quandary of Negro citizens in the state of Mississippi.

CHAPTER ONE

The Dark Roads of Equality

The dark side of Canton, Mississippi, was first exposed to me with the murder of Barbara Jean Brown, my sister.

Barbara Jean was born on December 25, 1947, in a small country township in Belzoni, Mississippi in Humphrey County. Her siblings were Bennie, Eliza and the twins, Mary and Susie. In 1956, Barbara Jean and her family moved from Belzoni, Mississippi to Madison County, and settled into their new home on the Graves' land.

Barbara Jean's parents were people who did their best to ensure that their family had the necessities of life. Her father, Joe, was a large, light complexioned man who stood six feet tall and weighed two hundred and eighty-two pounds. He was a firm man and raised his family on moral values, love for others, and the crops he grew. He got up early every morning, ate a hearty breakfast, and went out to feed their livestock.

Before leaving home for the cotton field every day, Joe would take a limb from a tree and brush away his footprints as he walked backward out of his yard. When he returned every night, he would always check to see if there were any additional footprints in the yard. He would also whistle as a sign that he was getting closer to the house. Joe was protective, and he was jealous.

Susie, our mother, was a dark complexioned woman of medium height who weighed one hundred sixty-five pounds. She did not work outside the home. Instead, she spent her time in her 'truck patch' raising sweet potatoes, peanuts, vegetables, and watermelon. In addition to growing all kinds of eateries for the family, she would spend her weekends washing clothes in an old washtub. I remember her dumping the clothes in a black iron pot and boiling them until the steam ascended high into the clouds. When the clothes had finished boiling, she removed them and dumped them into a washtub and hand-scrubbed every single garment with lye soap. Finally, she would twist the clothes by hand to remove all the water and then hang them on the cloth line to dry.

Back then, our home, like many others in our section of town, did not have indoor plumbing, electricity or heating unit. Father braved the cold weather to cut wood to burn to heat the home, and kerosene oil was used to light our rooms. The house did not have an indoor bathroom. So, my father carved a hole in the ground behind the house and built a wooden support structure around it, and called the structure an outhouse.

We did not have the conveniences of a modern home; either, but surrounded our home, we did have beautiful sunflowers plants, rose bushes, and lilies that mother had planted. We girls helped her water them and at nightfall in the summer, the penetrating fragrance from those flowers would fill the air as our family sat serenely on the front porch.

After his long days in the summer, when the sun stayed up until late in the night, my father would sit quietly in his favorite rocking chair smoking his rolled up Prince Albert cigarettes. One of our neighbors, Bad Eye, would come over with his family and swing back and forth in the swing we had. Soon he and father would be fast asleep.

The night was always welcome to our families because it gave us a chance to catch up on the local gossip and everything that was happening in town. Mother would sit there reading the Holy Scriptures and sometimes I would hear bits and pieces from my father and Bad Eye chitchat's about some men "messing" with the Negros in town.

Father was not a devout man, but he did take his family to church on Sunday in a horse-drawn buggy. On the first Sunday of every month at the Stokes Chapel Missionary Baptist Church, about twelve miles west of Canton, baptism was the custom and parishioners were baptized in the little fishing pond behind the church. Of course, many Negros did not own automobiles then, and most would walk to church because they all loved to hear Reverend J. B. Hart preach.

Reverend Hart, the Stokes Chapel pastor, was a brown complexioned, curly headed man who was only five foot, five, and weighed a scant one hundred fifty pounds, but he really could draw a crowd with his stirring messages and rousing baritone voice. Every first and third Sunday, the church was packed with women wearing big wide hats and men wearing worn out suits and unkempt shoes. Spiritual joy filled the interior of the wooden church as people focused on being their brothers' keepers while Desiree' Hart kicked off the song services by singing "When All of God's Children Get Together." The elderly mothers of the "motherboard", would follow with the old familiar hymn as "Give Me That Old Time Religion" or "At the Cross When I First Saw the Lord." What a time, what a time! I can see some of them now. Ms. Anthony, Gross, Bennett, Spencer, Luckett, Johnson, Brown, Kelly, Jackson, and so many more.

Toward the end of the summer, dreadfully, it was cotton season. Cotton was one of the main crops grown in the Madison County, so our family always worked our cotton field. No matter how hot the weather, father gathered the whole family and anybody else who could strap a sack on their backs, and we all went to the cotton field. The sacks were large enough to hold one hundred pounds of cotton per picker. Age was Not a factor. If the individual could walk, he or she could pick cotton from the sun up to dusk.

When the cotton sacks were full, father took the sacks to the baler for weighing. While cotton prices were higher per pound for the white folks, the baler's often cheated the Negros by paying them only two cents per pound.

In those days, it took one acre of cotton to fill a wagon that would make one bale of cotton. Imagine how long and hard the work was to earn enough money picking cotton for a family to buy one sack of flour.

Finally, when the cotton season was over, summer was ending too, and it was time to go back to school. Nothing could compare to the happy faces on us children when we saw the end of the cotton season.

The halls of the schoolhouse soon filled with children laughing, playing, and learning. My sister Barbara Jean and my brother Bennie were the only ones in our family then old enough to attend school. Mother made sure that Barbara Jean and Bennie ate a good breakfast before going off to school, and she also packed their lunches in tin pails filled with homemade teacakes and molasses. They were lucky if there were chickens in their pails.

Every day mother would walk the distance of ten miles round trip with Barbara Jean and Bennie over rough terrain, sometimes in the rain and cold, to the bus stop. The bus driver was Ms. Emma Jackson, (aka) Ms. Cat. Ms. Cat was a strict bus driver who ruled Highway 22. She did not allow loud noises, fighting, playing around, or standing on her bus. She was always focused on bus safety.

By 1959, my twin sister and I were finally ready for school. My little sister Carrie was born the same year. However, she was not born in a hospital because Negros was not allowed in hospitals then. A family friend who happened to be a midwife help birthed my little sister into the world, and she was the first breast-fed baby I had ever seen. I thought that this was so bizarre until mother explained that all of her children were fed that way. Carrie was a little princess even then and as the newest family member, she quickly learned how to get her way.

Barbara Jean, being the eldest, had to help with chores around the house and with taking care of Carrie. Barbara Jean loved helping out. She would change Carrie's Pampers and clothes. Did I say Pampers? At that time, Pampers was not available. The only diapers were rags, and all our clothes were homemade. Our family used every scrap we had to survive. Throwing nothing away.

As Susie Mae and I, the twins, were getting older, we got more curious. One day while poking around in father's work shed, Susie Mae found a bottle of cotton poison that he used to kill boll weevils in the cotton field. For some reason, she drank from the bottle and quickly became sick. My parents were frantic when they found her and the bottle together; her eyes closed, barely breathing. They believed their child was about to die. They took her to the King's Daughter hospital, but the hospital staff would not allow my parents in the front door of the hospital to see a doctor. We were Negros. My parents took her around to the back of the hospital where one doctor agreed to see her and flushed her stomach out. She went home feeling poorly, but alive.

Unlike, Susie Mae the only danger that I came close as a child was running in the mud with my shoes off. I loved the feel of mud between my toes. One day as I was playing in the mud, I accidentally stepped on a nail that went all the way through between the bones of my foot.

But father would not take me to the hospital he, instead, cut a piece of salt pork and wrapped the meat around the wound to draw out the infection. He refused to take me to the hospital because he did not want to go through the shame and humiliation of being denied again. Father was a proud, kind and gentle man, but the white folks for the most part had broken his spirit. The situation that he had encountered at the hospital with Susie Mae left him feeling less than a man when he was forced to take his child to the back of the hospital. Father felt that the staff at the hospital regarded his child's life as something less than a dog's. Susie Mae did not deserve to be in their all-inclusive white system. The experience took a toll on him and from that point on; many of his neighbors and close friends regarded his behavior as erratic and unpredictable, and some discarded him from their circle altogether.

I remember one time during one of father's bleaker moments when he wanted to wash Susie Mae's and my hair. He mixed a pot of hot water and ashes together in preparation for the washing and, gawking at us from across the yard, Barbara Jean knew that something was wrong. She ran to the house and called out for help and mother ran outside. She saw my father holding Susie Mae tightly to wash her hair. She called out to him, but she was ignored. Father then grabbed for me, but I ran into the cornfield for security. Almost immediately our neighbors came running and restrained him.

Father was taken to the hospital, and I did not see him again until five to six months later. The near-death experience of Susie Mae had finally gotten the best of him.

The rest of us had the innate ability and the support needed from neighbors to weather the storm of my father being away for such a long time. We looked to my mother to be the breadwinner, and she had to go to work to provide for us. It was hard during my father's absence. Usually we did not have enough to eat and went to bed hungrily.

On a cold winter morning, mother, being a survivor that she was, took a pair of my father's shoes and went to the pasture of the plantation owner. She singled out one of his cows, put the shoes on it, and guided the cow out of the pasture with my father's shoes on its hoofs so that no one could trace where the cow had gone. Mother took the cow to our shed where it was slaughtered and cured. We had food for days.

CHAPTER TWO

Love Thy Neighbors

Great Neighbors matter more than any tangible object on earth. The families that supported us during those terrible times while father was away became our extended family. The Butlers, Bennetts, Boltons, Jacksons, Nicholsons, and Bibbins all proved the value of friendship. They were the best. When one of them killed a hog or cow, we all shared in the feast.

The lives of the women in our families consisted to a large degree of making quilts and blankets, cooking, and gossiping. Young Barbara Jean would help the women make quilts by cutting out the swatches and stitching the pieces together. There was an art to making those quilts and blankets, and when the work was done, the women celebrated by cooking a huge meal of corn bread, greens, fried chicken, and blackberry cobbler. The men feasted on the scrumptious meals, too, while they gulped down glasses of sugar water.

One friend had a strange nickname, Bad Eye. Bad Eye was in his forties, was dark skinned and a large, strong man. He was an eccentric guy, and he kept to himself. Before father married mother, he and Bad Eye had been best friends. Though, that all changed after father brought his new wife and family to live on the Grave's place. Bad blood quickly snuck into that neighborly friendship.

Bad Eye must have liked looking at mother, and it seemed my father eyes soon began to wander in the opposite direction, toward Bad

Eye's wife. Who could blame either of them? They were both beautiful women.

During one hunting season, as my father prepared for the "big" rabbit hunt, Bad Eye's son Eddie asked father for a rabbit. Later that night, when father brought a rabbit back for him, he gave it to Bad Eye's wife, as Eddie wasn't there. Father didn't think at the time that there would be any problem with him giving the rabbit to Gladys. But there was.

Bad Eye thought that father had brought the rabbit only as a gift for his wife. Peace suddenly ceased to exist between us neighbors and within our friendly little community. It was like watching the Hatfield and McCoy fighting on a daily basis, except these men was Negros.

One beautiful spring evening, after the rain had stopped, father went to draw a bucket of water from the cistern and saw Bad Eye standing there at the side of the yard. Father, dropped his bucket, ran as fast as he could over to Bad Eye and hit him in the mouth. He knocked two of his teeth out. Bad Eye cussed something vicious and walked off, promising to get even.

Only much later did Bad Eye find out that the rabbit had been for his son. At this point, it did not matter to him, though, because my father had humiliated him in front of his family.

Bad Eye knew that father loved to drink on the weekends and that he had to pass his house to get home. One weekend, as my father was coming home from a night of drinking, Bad Eye was sitting on his front porch.

"Hey!" father called out. "I know you ain't sleeping'. You are playing' possum."

Father continued his name-calling and shouting just to get Bad Eye's attention. When father got closer, Bad Eye grabbed an axe from the side of the porch, ran over, and smacked father in the head. Blood went everywhere. That night, we all thought Joe was dead.

As soon as his health improved, of course, he vowed to get revenge.

From that day on, father started carrying a shotgun. That gun went everywhere he went, including the outhouse. That gun became his best friend.

Father fumingly wouldn't let go of his hostility. One-day father saw Bad Eye a ways up the road, just about to turn into his own yard. Father ducked behind a thick bush, and when Bad Eye crossed his path, he jumped out from behind the bush and hit him in the head with the barrel of the shotgun. This time the blood was Bad Eye's.

"Now, you so and so, I'm done," Joe said quietly.

These men were truly something else. Their relationship was so bad that the children could not play together. So, when they left, we played.

Our playtime in those days was not the average run-of-the-mill childhood playing. We played in the silo barns used to store silage for animals, and the cornfield was our imaginary sanctuary. We made dolls from corn stalks, the dolls' dresses from corn shucks, and the dolls' hair from the silk of the corn stalks. Our backyard was the kitchen where we used a black boiling pot for the stove. We made bread from the mud and cut up greens from the grass.

When it came time for summer fun, we did not go to the big cities and slide down the huge water slides. Our summer pastime was fishing in the pond behind the house.

One day as we were fishing, our little sister, unbeknownst to us, walked too close to the side of the pond and fell in. Terrified, Barbara Jean, ran for help. She came across Theodore, Bad Eye's oldest son, and called out to him for help. He ran to the pond and saved our little sister from drowning.

When father and mother came home and heard what had happened, they whipped the shaving out of us with a "Piss Allen" switch. Those switches do not bend or break. They're designed for pain.

Moments later, my parents called us together again and talked to us about the importance of maintaining the security of the family. They said it was our responsibility to see that no harm came to the smallest ones.

"If one gets hurt, we all hurt," mother told us. *"If one goes missing, we all lose."*

CHAPTER THREE

Family Matters

Families were more devoted back then to each other because love and caring for one's brothers and sisters meant something. Ours was a large, loving family. On my father side of the family, the men were light complexioned, but they had one sister whose skin tone was dark. My mother's family was dark skinned, and they were the descendants of the Black Crow Indians.

My grandmother on my father's side was Sallie, a no nonsense woman who approached life in that same manner. She had worked for years as a maid for the Graves' family who owned the land my father farmed. When my father married his dark skinned wife, my mother, Sallie was livid. Grandma did not like dark skinned people even though she was dark skinned herself.

Grandma even treated her dark skinned grandchildren differently from those whose skin tones were fairer. She'd give the fair-skinned grandchildren yummy treats and would allow them to play in the house, especially her bedroom. Those grandchildren with darker skin tones did not get treats and could not play in that unique room. It was a place reserved only for those fair-skinned children and grandchildren. Grandma allowed me to play there, although, at the time, I did not understand why.

That room was fit for a queen. It was filled with priceless figurines, white lace curtains, and antiques and I remember there was one little brown box on top of the dresser with a beautiful ballerina inside. When the box pop opened, the figure would pop out and danced. I was in heaven watching, it.

I loved Grandma's bedroom. The crisp smell of mothballs and linen filled the air. Her bed was made of solid wood and covered with a medallion white chenille bedspread with a basket pattern stitched and woven into the middle, and it had delicate twisted decorative edges all around the bottom. Her sheets were pure white, starched and perfectly ironed. The wooden floors were always shined to a gloss. Everything about that room was amazing. It was an irreplaceable place, a place to escape my everyday life and enter into a world of beauty.

My Grandma was not a kind woman, though. I should make that clear. She was a sometimes-cantankerous woman who did not take kindly to certain people, and her dislike of Susie, my mother, now stands to reason. I can chuckle now, thinking about Grandma and Susie fighting, but in those days, when I was only four or five, their yelling at each other scared me. Grandma wanted to control Susie and her family, and not only was the color of Susie's skin irritating to Grandma, but Grandma also couldn't stand the fact that she was never able to exercise control over Susie.

Grandma was a busybody, too. She always had her nose in other people's business, whether invited or not. One Sunday morning, my sister Barbara Jean was getting ready for church, and she forgot to put on a slip. Grandma had a hissy melt down. She and Barbara Jean ended up "discussing" the matter loudly in church, and they caused a horrible disturbance. My Grandma believed that young women should always wear slips and if they did not, they were considered floozies. My mother felt the same way. I don't know if Barbara Jean herself ended up being convinced, though.

When it came down to how the Ushers should conduct themselves during the church service Grandma and my mother had difference opinions. Because my mother was the president of the ushers, and-Grandma was the vice-president. My Grandma wanted the ushers to greet preachers and visitors a certain way when they entered the sanctuary, and my mother thought that the Ushers should treat them in a different way. The only person that I felt sorry for at this point, though, was Barbara Jean because she was the one doing the usher work. Once again, she was caught between these two domineering women.

As the first-born child, Barbara Jean had a lot on her plate. Father always encouraged her, though. He would tell her, "Stay in school. Learn all you can, and help your sisters and brother."

It was hard on my brother growing up in father's house because he did not receive favorable treatment. My brother received only harsh treatment, basically, because Joe was not his father. In fact, father had no love for him at all, but he needed the extra help with the farm, feeding the livestock and doing chores around the house.

One warm, rainy afternoon, my sister Barbara Jean saw father-whipping Bennie with a belt made from a piece of rawhide. Father was angry about something and decided to take it out on my brother. When Barbara Jean confronted father, he became angrier and told her, *"You stay out of my business!"*

She only wanted to know why father was so angry and what had happened to make him take it out on our brother. After father had shrieked loudly at her, she ran to ask our mother what was going on, but the only reply there was, *"That is your daddy's business."*

I felt ashamed of my father's treatment of Bennie, and I wanted to hit him myself. I never did, of course, but after that day, my sister Barbra Jean would shout, loudly, at him, of course under her breath. She had begun to sense more deeply the ill treatment our brother received, and she would talk relentlessly about social changes that would improve the inequality and eliminate the injustice for all people.

The fight for justice began in our home. The fight for equality for Bennie made a lasting impression on her, and she told me she had vowed to stop injustice by any means necessary. But, she said, she really did not know what to do. She only knew that equal justice mattered.

Dismayed over the occurrences that were going on with her family, Barbara Jean remained optimistic. She concentrated her angry in her studies. She was an outstanding student at the Cameron Street Negro Elementary School from 1956 to 1958, where Professor C. W. High was the school principal. Prior to attending Cameron, she had been a student at the McNeil Elementary School for Negros (1952-1956) in Humphrey County.

Professor C. W. High, the principal at Cameron Street Negro Elementary School, was a stern man who loved his Negro schoolchildren, and he tried to do the best for them. One school day while Barbara Jean was standing outside the schoolyard buying chocolate milk, Professor High came up to her.

"Brown, better get to class, better get to class," he said. She ran as fast as she could to be on time for class.

Every day Professor High greeted the schoolchildren over the intercom, *"Good morning boys and girls. We are happy to have you at school today."* He always made the day easier and brighter for his schoolchildren.

In 1958, Barbara Jean transferred to the Color Elementary School for Negros where Mrs. Ethel Nichols was the school principal. In 1959, the school name was changed to Roger Elementary School. Barbara Jean then transferred from the Cameron Street Elementary Negro School because the superintendent of schools closed the school and transferred all students to Rogers Middle School at the end of the school term. Barbara Jean was eleven years old and in the six-grade.

She was a tremendous student at her new school, as well. From the age of twelve through fourteen years old, however, she had grown tired of the overused books that were handed down from the white public schools. She had become fed up, too, with the substandard educational curriculum that may have been "applicable" for Negro students, but had no use for future earnings. The Negro school did not offer classes in physics, calculus, foreign language, or college prep courses like the white public schools all did.

Barbara Jean began to speak to the school officials – sometimes quite loudly about the need to improve the quality of education and the resources at her school. Mrs. Nichols, the principal, considered her a radical and a troublemaking student who also was making trouble for the other students. Barbara Jean did learn the curriculum, but that did not mean that she was satisfied.

In the meantime, during the early spring of that year, violence had begun to snake its way through the streets of Canton as Negros challenged the status quo of white control. The word of the Lord says, "Love hides a multitude of faults," but no one had apparently encouraged Deputy Sheriff Dick Stone and Constable Hervey Evans to hear those words before they raided Alex Johnson home on April 16th for suspicion of having illegal alcohol. Johnson was a member of the NAACP.

His home was searched, but the two officers only found a brown bag with a bottle of whiskey in it. Constable Evans and Deputy Sheriff Stone placed Johnson under arrest anyway. Then Constable Evans shot Johnson once in the chest. He died just outside the door of his home, still in handcuffs.

Medgar Evers heard about this, and he instituted a full-scale discovery about the vicious police brutality in Johnson's death. At an advisory committee meeting, Evers presented three affidavits showing a "wanton type of police brutality" in the death of Alex Johnson. Murray Cox, the committee chairman, only replied, *"The affidavits would be forwarded to the commission."*

There was never another mention about the subject.

At about the same time Aaron Henry of Clarksdale, chairman of the Regional Council of Negro Leadership, made a partial report to the same committee about why so few Negros voted in Mississippi.

"Of the forty-eight districts that I have visited," he said, *"the chief reasons why Negros do not show up to take the voter registration are their fear of failure, economic reprisals, and physical harm. There's apathy among the Negros and insufficient encouragement by Negro leaders."*

Police corruption continued. It was business as usual.

William Smith, Jr., was accused of raping a white girl, fifteen-year-old Elise Goober, after she had reported that he had raped her. She said that she was parked in a car with her boyfriend, seventeen-year-old James Myers, when they smelled whiskey coming through the open window of the car door. Then Smith opened the car door, pulled a knife on her and her boyfriend, and made them walk to a nearby cornfield, where he had raped her.

The Justice Department hired attorney Jack Graves to represent Smith in the rape case because it was alleged that Sheriff Billy Noble had beaten a confession from Smith and that the girl and her seventeen-year-old boyfriend had lied.

In the fall of 1962, Barbara Jean's life was about to change. At the age of fifteen, she enrolled in school at the Rogers Junior Senior Color High School and the radical and troublemaker label given to her by her former principal followed her to junior-senior high. Mr. James Jones was a high school principal. He was short, the overweight dark-skinned man who was a timid little guy and, in my opinion, was afraid of white folks.

Barbara Jean was tall, 5'11", and weighed one hundred and thirty pounds. She had brown eyes and brownish black hair. She liked wearing her hair pinned up with hair bows, and she loved wearing bobby socks, polished shoes, and skirts above her knees. She was an avid reader.

One day as she was reading, she came across an old 1958 news article in the *Madison County Herald* newspaper about her school, Rogers Junior-Senior Color High. Many of the white citizens had been receiving accolades for placating the Negro citizens of Madison County by recognizing the 1954 Supreme Court decision Brown v. Board of Education. The study suggested that some of the white citizens were doing their best to protect their seclusion from the detrimental effects of those who might inhabit their space. Negros, in other words. Building a new junior-senior colored high school for the Negros on acres of land near the same area of the old junior-senior colored school was their quick remedy.

The new school, Barbara Jean noted, had fifteen classrooms, an auditorium, a gymnasium, a cafeteria, and ancillary building, but the elementary and the new high school were combined in the same building with classrooms for each on separate wings of the school. The news article also said that the cost to build the school had an "enormous price tag" of two hundred and fifty thousand dollars. It was an honor, though, to read that the newly constructed building was named in honor of her new principal A. M. Rogers.

The town had a big dedication ceremony to honor Principal Rogers. He showed his appreciation for the honor, and he seemed gratified, but privately he seemed frightened by it.

"When one receives such praises," he said, *"it pushes them up the ladder, and the higher one gets up that ladder, the harder the fall is when one does not measure up."*

Despite the new school and Principal Rogers received endearing tributes that day, there were mixed emotions and feelings on the part of some, particularly the NAACP Field Secretary Medgar Evers. Members of the National Association for the Advancement of Colored People were concerned because the "new" school looked like an auction barn that was overcrowded, and they said it was unsuitable for education.

"I understand that the school was a last-minute compromise to conciliate Negro people," Medgar Evers said, "and that it was created as an answer to the Supreme Court decision of 1954 to keep segregation in the white school. The new Negro junior-senior high school of Madison County is ill-equipped and overtaxed with students, has the striking resemblance of an auction barn, and is inadequate to provide for each child the maximum educational opportunity that this day and age demand. The Negro citizens will not accept as satisfactory this last minute, makeshift school program. Those Negros who aid in keeping other Negros in the deplorable conditions under which we live in Mississippi should be singled out for who they are, profiteers at the inhuman expense of their fellow man."

The new Negro school was considered the largest institution of its kind at that time and the embodiment of Negro education in Mississippi, if one could believe that. The outcome of biracial planning to continue the segregation of Madison County schools was about to change, though.

The leading county watchdog committee, the White Citizens' Council, worked frantically to play down the NAACP statements, and they petitioned the city and school officials of Canton to appeal to the Negros and encourage them to accept their new school for a new means to educate. Their informants, Reverend H. H. Humes, the editor of the Negro newspaper of Greenville, Mississippi, and Percy Green, the editor of the *Jackson Advocate* newspaper were both contacted by the state watchdog committee, the Mississippi Sovereignty Commission, that paid them to emerge publicly as friends of the NAACP, but within the Negro community to learn the movements of the NAACP.

Mayor Andrew Simpson of Canton was also contacted, and he wrote a story in the *Madison County Herald* newspaper counteracting Evers' statements. "The Negros appear to be well content with their new public *school. In addition, we have built them a new swimming pool and A. M. Rogers, the principal of the Negro school, is a dependable Negro."*

The Canton public school superintendent, Robert Cox, also refuted Evers' charges.

"This is not the truth," he said. *"The school is not overcrowded. The endorsed report presented from the board of trustees revealed that Negro students' enrollment is up. In fact, the enrollment count is over one thousand, which is an average daily attendance of over eight hundred. The class load is only twenty-six students per teacher, even if not all of them are in a class at the same time. Yet I must stress that these classrooms do not include audio-visual equipment and music rooms or a manual arts workshop. Nonetheless, they are acceptable."*

In an even more extreme measure to placate the Negro community and show support of the school problem, the associate editor for the *Madison County Herald* newspaper, Phil Mullen, placed an ad in the newspaper to steer attention away from Evers' comments. The ad read, *"It is not education the NAACP wants. Clearly, the NAACP is saying that this school, built mostly with the white taxpayers' money, is not adequate because white children do not attend. Yet some thirty-seven teachers, all from the high school, have endorsed the new facility."* The endorsed list of teachers is Johnnie Ruth Brown, Margaret W. Brumfield, Marie Cole, Annie S. Crawford, Coleman Garrett, and Wallace E. Green, James Albert Hill, Eugene Jackson, Nathan Jackson, Dannie B. Jones, Dorothy L. Jones, T. H. Jones, Pauline G. Jordan, Sarah T. McCaskill, Cordelia J. McNeal, Ethel L. Nichols, Harold Thigpen, Josipearl Williams, Doris J. Loach, and Mamie B. Williams. In addition, teachers from the Junior High School were Clemetean Archie, Hattie C. Barron, Elease R. Blackman, Lillian G. Boyd, Lessie P. Branson, Eunice D. Coldwell, Laura B. Davis, Marie Douglas, Gracie S. Green, Bessie T. Robinson, Nina P. Stewart, Ida Mae Stokes, Warren C. Stringfellow, Virginia J. Whitehead, and

Mozelle Williams. *"All of these teachers have expressed their appreciation for the new facilities,"* Mullen wrote. On the other hand, not published, those teachers' resources had been endangered; consequently, they had to corporate with the school officials and agreed to the content of the article to keep their jobs.

These intimidation tactics were not enough to stop the strong-minded Negro students from seeking a better education with functioning learning equipment and material. In fact, the activities of so many to "improve the situation" of the Negro school were a great disappointment. The students were still dissatisfied with the substandard, hand-me-down books and the non-operational lab equipment, unlike what was available to the white public school students. The white schools also offered their student's curricula that were designed to prepare them for the future.

Barbara Jean felt that the school system had purposely botched the learning opportunities for all Negro students, and she did not hesitate to voice those feelings. In an effort to bring down the walls of injustice and inequity, one day she and a handful of students staged a school walkout in protest of the deplorable educational conditions at their school. Not only did the group fight against the asymmetrical educational system in their school, but they also protested the lack of representation for all Negro citizens in Madison County.

Barbara Jean felt that if the Negros had higher state and local representation, as well as representation in Congress, things would be better. But she needed help in putting the pieces together. She went to her mother, Susie Brown, who was already an active member in the local NAACP branch, in Canton. Susie told Barbara Jean about Medgar Evers and the work he was doing as the Field Secretary for the NAACP and how, in 1960, he had launched student-centered auxiliaries in other districts and influenced students from Jackson, Campbell, and Tougaloo Colleges to join the movement against inequality. She also explained how Medgar organized students in one metropolitan county to boycott some of the white-established businesses, and how some students tested the United States Supreme Court decision banning segregation in federal interstate transportation by riding the Trailways and Greyhound buses.

At this point, Susie and Barbara Jean became convinced that Medgar Evers were the right person to organize their local group. Additional expertise also became available to the students from Clarence O. Chinn, Clearance O. Chinn, Jr., Walter Small, Gabe Davis, Carrie Smoot, John W. Mills, John Brown, Wilbert Robinson, George Washington, Minnie Lou Chinn, James Collier, Henry Chinn, Thaddeus Hewitt, Levy Jackson, and George T. Raymond to name a few. The Ladner sisters, Doris and Joyce, were immense supporters of the Canton youth movement.

The Youth Civil Rights Movement of Madison County was born. They centered their attention on quality education, better school equipment, resources, and equality for all people. When Medgar Evers came to Canton, he was able to help form an unwavering student coalition in Madison County.

As a young nine-year-old Negro child growing up in Canton, I knew that being part of a revolution of this magnitude was going to be an eye opening experience that would never happen again in my lifetime. It was breathtaking to witness Negros supporting each other in the mission of the movement.

Medgar Evers and Susie Brown, by then both veteran civil rights activists, knew that their job would not be easy. The White Citizen's Council of Madison County quickly learned of Medgar Evers' presence in Canton through one of their informants, Percy Green, and placed Evers under continual surveillance.

Evers never stopped working with the youth of Canton. He also invited the Jackson Student Non-Violence Coordinating Committee (SNCC) leader, James Collier, to help the youth organize an SNCC branch in Canton.

Barbara Jean became an active member of this branch, and she became involved with activities of the Congress On Racial Equality (CORE), too. Barbara Jean worked for the SNCC distributing information about the SNCC and CORE projects in the community.

CORE became the pivotal group in the civil rights movement. Their purposes in Canton were to get Negros to register to vote, to establish a community center, a library, and to begin reading and typing classes for practical use for the future of Negro children.

The students' first mission was to improve the quality of education at their new school. They realized, with the assistance of CORE, that the real starting point to develop future education was going to be integration.

CHAPTER FOUR

Integration: A Tough Nut to Crack

The 1962 integration would be a geographical as well as a social challenge because Canton was a divided town with Negros on the west and white folks on the east. CORE members were determined, though, to end segregation in Canton public schools, communities, restaurants, buses, bathrooms, water fountains, and other city venues.

In those days, downtown, Canton was a scene from one of Norman Rockwell's paintings. It still is, to a large degree. The main thoroughfare to downtown Canton was and is Peace Street. It leads right to the town square and the Madison County Courthouse; a large, intimidating brown and white building adorned with four large white columns, a super round dome on top, four walkway entrances, and a well-manicured lawn.

In the early sixties the stores that lined Peace Street were Mosby Drugs, Stanley, TWL, Guys Drugs, Buttress, Iupe Fair, Sterling, Ben Franklin, Fred's Dollar Store, Price Lewis Gas Station, Gowdy Jewelers, a radio station and a doctor's office with segregated patients' waiting room. Across the square were the A.Saab, Buttress, and Hancock stores. On the west side of the square were the movie theater, Wardell's Restaurant and Mecca Cafe. The east side of Canton housed the affluent homes on East Fulton, East Academy, Madison and Priestly streets; all steeped in their antebellum style and tradition, along with the prestigious white Canton High and Elementary Schools. The west side of

Canton housed the town's poorer homes on West Fulton, West Academy, Lutz and Franklin streets while first and second avenues were steeped in shaky shotgun houses, some without indoor toilets. Slum areas lined the railroad tracks and spread westward to the lagoon, all unenviable places to live. The Joe Preacher Home, otherwise known as the projects, and the Negro Rogers High and Elementary Schools also lay on the west side of town. There were only a few Negro homes on that side of Canton that could be classified as decent.

CORE knew it was time to tear down the walls that separated the west from the east and put into effect the Supreme Court ruling of Brown vs. the Board of Education. Gaining release from the chain of partition and the fixed ideas of the Canton school officials would be a tough nut to crack, we knew, and there had already been more than sixty years of desegregation running through each of the combatant's veins. No one was about to lie down without a fight.

What sensible man could blame Negros for feeling overjoyed that the Supreme Court had announced that Negro children could go to the same schools as white children? It was not a privilege, but a moral and legal right we now had to enjoy. Was it not a God given right, as well, to enjoy the same quality of education as others? We said, *"Yes, why not!"*

Of course, this was easier said than done because the strongest supremacy group in Canton, the White Citizens' Council, was not about to give up its years of generational roots imbedded deep within the walls of the divide.

It would also be a misconception to think that this change was going to happen overnight in Madison County. No, this was a fireball rolling faster and faster down the hill. I waited, in all of my eleven-year-old glory, at the bottom of that hill along with my sister Barbara Jean to see where the burning residue would land.

The county watchdog group took a fight or flight stance against school integration. They fought this problem with all of their might and money, but could not stop the civil rights movement to integrate the schools.

Our founding ancestors were forced into this country as an indifferent nation and found cynicism, fear, and narrow-mindedness of some who would refuse a child the right to an education. Following in those discriminatory footsteps, the Canton City officials, in their effort to deter any civil rights activities in Canton, instituted a citywide alert for information leading to the arrest of any agitators, troublemakers, or subversive groups stirring up trouble.

Prior to the arrival of SNCC and CORE, Sheriff Marion Simpson was not sure if there were any Negros trying to integrate white schools. Barbara Jean had been labeled a troublemaker by the principal, but that alarm may never have sounded in the mayor's office. The sheriff was soon enlightened, though, about the current unrest by one of his informants, H. A. Jones, a forty-seven year old Negro male who lived in Canton and worked for a burial association as an insurance agent.

The White Citizens' Council, too, was becoming increasingly on edge to find out as much as possible about the school integration movement in Madison County. By this time, there were integration cases pending before the Supreme Courts of Kansas, South Carolina, Virginia, and Delaware where Negro students had admonished the "Separate, but Equal" policy in Plessey vs. Ferguson. The Canton White Citizens' Council did not want to be blindsided by a case of their own. In their minds, the Ferguson case was already a tenable foundation to exclude Negros from attending the white public schools.

At that time, Editor Mullen, with the *Madison County Herald* Newspaper, published an article that read,

"The good Negros everywhere in the south should get away from the NAACP, an organization that is not for Negros but for the destruction of America and supported by the President of the United States and the Warren court. Work with the white people in maintaining good race relations because when integration occurs in schools, it is the Negro teachers who are relieved of their jobs and not the white teachers. The Negros should also ponder and weigh soundly in Little Rock because many Negro children had become pawns of the NAACP. Private schools will replace public schools in order to maintain segregation and the private schools are for the white children."

In the meantime, Horace Germany a 6'1", 190 pounds, black hair, blue eyes, and ruddy complexion white preacher man from Decatur, Mississippi wanted to establish a school in Canton for Negro preachers. So, Germany took four Negro men to a White Citizens Council meeting to get approval for the school. Reports showed when they arrived, the committee representative Walter Ray met them at the door and told Germany, *"It is okay for you to come into the building but not the four niggers."* So, Germany went in alone. However, the school was not approved, but Germany was told to get out of town in ten days.

Ray then instructed Sheriff Marion Simpson to contact some of his deputies to investigate the owners of the cars seen parked at Germany home. One of those cars were a 1979 Plymouth wagon. The car was registered to Renfroe grocery store owner who alleged that his wife allowed the cook to use the car for errands. Though, he was not aware that the car was used to transport Naggers to an NAACP meetings.

Days later, Germany learned that more guests had been spied on including getting threaten phone calls himself. He was brutally beaten. With cows poisoned, the barn burned, and threats to his father's life, Germany refused to abandon his dream to build the Negro school for preachers.

Not giving up, Germany called a press conference as he was not able to depend on the FBI for any help. He reported to the local newspaper, saying:

"To be very frank about it all, those who are fighting so gallantly for segregation have more to fear from equality than from integration. I speak as a southerner, born and reared in the South. Therefore, I have some access to the picture as it stands. Let us go back to the start of it all. The Negro was brought to this county by white men to be their slave and to wait on them; complacency of this period went well for a while, and no Negro slave would dare to compare himself with his master. Finally, some whites saw the evil of this well-established custom and broke rank with it. Slavery began to be looked upon with disfavor. Men, through the fear of God and respect for humanity, white and black, began to spearhead a movement to free the slaves because slavery was contrary to Christian principles. The fear behind this fear is that a freed Negro meant that the master would have to accept the fact that he was no longer the master and the Negro his slave; they would then be on bargaining terms. The master would be master no longer, unless he could bluff the former slave into humility and subdue him through fear."

Germany continues to receive threats. His mail was scrutinized to determine whether he was receiving mail from the NAACP. He was also beaten again, however, this time to the point of death.

Now fearing for his and his father's life, Germany contacted John Buehler one of his white friends for help. Buehler wrote a letter to Governor Ross Barnett about the circumstances that his friend had encountered in Canton. The letter read,

"I am sure that you do not personally think that the Negros should not have a trained ministry for their people. Certainly, there is no better way to help the Negro than to provide for his spiritual needs. As one man said to me in Meridian, 'We teach them to jump in Mississippi, but some day they will be making us jump.' Whether we like it or not, the whole world is on the move

and the events of the past fifteen years show us that the movement is rapid. Unless we come to grips with the situation in the next fifteen years, the dark skinned people of the world that outnumber us four to one might inundate the white race. I can see no better way to meet this problem than to train Negro preachers who will in turn go to their people with the message of Christ."

The plot against Negros thickens as the watchdog committee continued to collect information about the school integration. So, different interviews were conducted with the Negro school administrators. Kirby Walker, the director of the colored schools, was the first one to be interviewed. Followed by James Goodloe the principal of Velma Jackson School and Laverne Randolph to determine the degree of their knowledge concerning the integration.

If they had the knowledge, they did not or were not willing to share it with them.

But, nonetheless, the watchdog committee was not about to give up. They were ruthless to fight against integration by any means, so they contacted the superintendent (Cox) of the public schools for answers. On the other hand, he volunteered that he knew of no Negro students trying to integrate the white schools.

However, unbeknownst to them, Reverend Johnson, a thirty-seven year-old white missionary from Detroit, Michigan; sympathetic to the Negros' dilemma was in Canton to support integration. He attended the Negro churches around Canton. On one occasion, Reverend Johnson and his family went to the Rising Star Negro Church on Robinson Road, about eight miles east of Canton. When he arrived at the church, he and his family walked to the front of the church and sat down. The Negros sitting on those seats automatically stood up and walked to the back of the church.

Reverend Johnson got up, walked to the back of the church, and told the Negros, *"Move up front with my family. You are as good as we are."*

The Negros moved, and Reverend Johnson gained their respect and loyalty.

Soon, Reverend Johnson began fearing for the safety of his family because he attended Negro churches and asked Sheriff Marion Simpson for protection. Reverend Johnson had been getting threats from a group of white men shouting to take matters into their own hands if he did not get out of town or stop socializing with niggers.

Sheriff Simpson would not provide any protection for Johnson. Instead, he tried to put a stop to Johnson because he said Johnson was putting his family in danger.

W. A. Graves, Johnson's friend, was a white informant for the Sheriff's Department. One day he provoked Johnson into a fight by claiming that he was talking crazy talk about integrating the Negro churches and the white public schools.

"I went to Little Rock, Arkansas," Graves said, "to visit relatives, and when I came home, I told Reverend Johnson about my visit. I said to him, "I think that the Negros in Arkansas have stopped trying to integrate the schools there."

"No, they have not stopped," Johnson told him. "In Arkansas the people are just like the people in Mississippi, a group of cheap politicians, and this is the reason the country is in the shape it is today."

Graves became angry and bellowed, "If you do not change your ways, somebody is going to knock those big rimmed glasses off your face!"

"Nobody is going to bother me," Johnson said, "because the NAACP and the FBI are behind me."

Then Graves did just what he had told Reverend Johnson that somebody would do and knocked his glasses off his face.

In the midst of everything that was going on in Canton, another violent tragedy surfaced when Joe Brown, Barbara Jean's father, was found hanging from a tractor near his home just ten miles west of Canton. Joe's death was the quiet before the storm because it set the motion of events in Barbara Jean's life for the next two years. Joe had gotten up early that morning, as he always did, except this morning he was dead, at the age of forty-nine, in the field ten miles west of Canton.

Sheriff Billy Noble and the FBI were called. After the Sheriff had arrived and conducted a "quickie" investigation into the death, he concluded, *"Though we still are checking on the experience of the death, I am inclined to believe that it is a suicide."*

Sheriff Noble was in his thirties was about 5'9", and weighed two hundred and ninety pounds. In the opinion of many, he was the meanest, low down, dirty dog of a sheriff to walk the grounds of Madison County. The Sheriff could have cared less about my father's death because he had a deep hatred for Negros, to him, it was one less nigger to contend with in Canton.

The family did not understand or accept suicide as a cause of death because father loved life and his family. When mother went to the crime scene, she saw her husband of over twenty years hanging from his tractor. His gun was in a place where it looked like he had been trying to reach for it, but could not grasp it. He did not have on his shoes, and his body appeared to have been messed with. She knew Joe did not kill himself and leave his children.

Mother spoke to Sherriff Noble and, based on her assumption, the Sheriff then spoke too many of his neighbors and to the tobacco chewing plantation owner. The investigation became a dead end, though, because there was no autopsy performed on the body, and there were no witnesses.

In those days, our family was powerless to do anything else.

Nevertheless, integration was making some progress, but violence was making more. On April 5th, county Constable Hervey Evans was patrolling an area within the Negro community when he came across two Negro males. One of the men was Booker Johnson of Walnut Street, a known advocate of the NAACP. The constable led Johnson to his patrol car and hit him after pushing him into the back seat. He then started to chase the other man, who was too afraid to give his name, but he was able to run away.

Constable Evans then went to the home of Judge Milton Sandige, a Justice of the Peace Judge, to file an affidavit against Johnson for public drunkenness. The judge issued the warrant and escorted Constable Evans to Johnson's home to arrest him. It was unique, to say the least, for a Justice Court judge to go to help arrest an alleged lawbreaker when he would be the same judge who would try the case.

When the two of them arrived, Johnson was in bed. To prevent any disturbance in the neighborhood, the Constable informed Johnson's neighbors that he was being arrested for being drunk in public and not for being drunk in his home. It was not against the law to drink in one's home, but was against the law to drink in public because Madison County was a dry county back then.

The two officials arrested Booker Johnson, but when they had driven about a quarter of a mile from Johnson's home, Johnson grabbed the constable by the back of his shirt collar and said, "*I am the wrong Negro.*"

Constable Evans stopping the car quickly, the two men struggled, and Constable hit the Negro in the head several times with the butt of his pistol. He was stunned by the injuries and was then taken straight to jail.

Constable Evans needed to keep this incident quiet, especially from the NAACP, but the NAACP did get wind of the subject because

Johnson was released into the custody of a friend who took him to report the incident to the Civil Rights Advisory Committee.

The NAACP then began a massive campaign to fight against the brutality, injustice, and covert surveying against all Negros. They contacted many new ministers in the area to use their churches as new locations to hold their meetings.

They ended up being blindsided, though, by one Negro informant, Walter Paden, who informed the chief of police about the NAACP's plan. The chief asked for help from other authorities in maintaining security in his city because his department was small and in the event that trouble began in Canton; he said, "*I need the extra fire power to maintain law and order.*"

The chief was confident that he would know whether any trouble was going to take place in Canton because his Negro informant Walter Paden would let him know. Constable Evans boldly summed the situation up.

"*I appreciate all the interests who are helping our township,*" he said, "*but I intend to enforce the law and will not tolerate any violence by hotheads or agitators that might be connected with the NAACP group. I am also sure that I have the support of all the good citizens of Madison County in regards to keeping law and order. I am a member of the White Citizens' Council. The council and I work hand-in-hand regarding any trouble caused by this subversive group or by any foreign agitators who plan to disrupt the activities of law abiding citizens.*"

The White Citizens' Council was doing everything within their power to defeat the mission of the CORE group and they finally raided the Freedom House where the CORE members lived and trashed it inside. Barbara Jean was working as a field worker for the company. She had always spoken her mind, at home, at school, and now in the town, but she was not alone. Carole Merritt, Claude Weaver, Andrew Lee Green, and many others also needed to improve the economic and social opportunities for Negros in her school and remove the stigma of injustice. None of them was in the Freedom House during the raid because they were out in the field distributing leaflets.

Up to this point, Barbara Jean had not realized that her involvement would encounter risks of the magnitude of the raid, but she did not abandon the cause.

In fact, Barbara jean and her friends went about their lives as usual while still handing out leaflets about integration and the white business boycotts. They knew the school prom was coming up, and she and her friends began to gather the materials they needed to make their prom dresses.

They went into the Hancock Fabric Store to buy fabric, but when they entered the store, the store clerk did not offer to help them. Instead, they were asked to leave. The group went to other stores in town only to endure the same treatment. By the time they had gone into and were booted out of T.W.L., Iupe Fair, Stanley, Fred's Dollar Store, and Sterling, they found out that the same discriminatory practices were going on in every business in Canton.

They started to investigate for themselves other businesses in town, including the Greyhound bus depot. This was another segregation issue all to itself, as the Negros were always compelled to sit in the back of the bus or give up their seats to the whites when the bus was full.

They found that there was also widespread exclusion from the white movie theater in town and the surrounding towns. They had no problem in buying their movie tickets. The problem was that after they had bought their tickets, they could not go into the same seating area that their white peers could. They had to go to the back of the theater to sit in seats reserved for "Colored." Negros was separate and not equal.

Barbara Jean was enraged.

CHAPTER FIVE

Economic Power:
Don't Buy at those Stores

On January 10, 1963, the NAACP organized a meeting at the Pleasant Green Christ Holiness Church to discuss the boycott's next line of attack. It was a frigid night, but hundreds of Negro members showed up and young people ranging in age from nine to fifteen and wearing CORE T-shirts were coming through the doors. This was the largest audience yet.

George Raymond, a Negro male in his twenties who sported a neatly trimmed beard, was the keynote speaker. The meeting kicked off with scriptures and prayers read by many ministers and by what had by now become the Negro national song, *"We Shall Overcome."* Raymond went over the purposes for the meeting and discussed the plan for the voter registration and boycotts. The primary stratagem was to get the attention of the powers-to-be, and the best method of getting their attention, Raymond said, was through a countywide boycott.

Raymond knew there would be a great deal of danger in this, and possibly even more deaths, but he explained we needed the most effective means to hit them where it most hurt: their wallets. The other speakers included Robert Moses, James T. McCain, Donald White, David Ellis, Jessie Harris, James Jones, Charles Cobb, and Art Thomas of the National Council of Churches. Art Thomas explained that he was going to ask the

Northern Presbyterian Ministers to come to Canton for the demonstration because their participation would justify federal intervention.

At the end of the meeting, Raymond spoke again. He stressed that there would be three thousand or more people in Canton to help organize the boycott and the Freedom Day activities. He stressed the importance, too, of the voter wide registration rally that was already scheduled in Madison County.

""*Everyone be calm,*" he said, "*but if the policemen want to get tough, we can get tough to. We are not afraid.*"

The meeting ended with McCullough motivating the people with the objectives and the accomplishments of the CORE group, and he spoke of the need for all of us to support the group. Jim, a white male from New York, accentuated McCullough's remarks by saying we should all stand strong in support of CORE because only by working together can we all win. Raymond then recruited additional CORE members.

The meeting was uplifting and informative, and people left feeling hopeful. They did believe that the goal to start the boycott could be successful if we worked together.

The NAACP, still continually harassed by the police, typically met two times per week at different churches in Canton. The most conspicuous places were the Mount Pleasant Baptist Church, Mount Zion Baptist Church, Saint Paul Church, Mount Pleasant Christ Holiness Church, and Liberty Baptist Church. Police officers were at every meeting. They wrote down the license plate numbers to get the names and addresses of every person in attendance. They took snapshots, listened from outside the building with electronic snooping devices, stopped cars, and then followed the attendees' home.

Because the police officers had gotten names and addresses, some of the NAACP conference attendees lost their jobs. Others were arrested for violations that were never considered necessary before the movement.

It also became a common occurrence for Negros to be whipped with si-phon hoses and nightsticks. Some were even killed.

To ensure some security of the people, the President of the United States finally sent armed federal troops to Canton. Their orders were to bring peace and to exercise justice for the Negro children trying to integrate the white public schools as well as for those individuals who wanted to participate in the voter registration meetings and rallies.

Thirty days later, on February 10, the members of National Council of Churches were able to attend a meeting at the Saint Paul Church on Franklin Street. Over one hundred people came. The keynote speaker, Elton Cox, a young man with CORE, told the group he would be out front, *"up close and personal,"* to lead the march to the courthouse. He would have an eighty-two year old Negro woman leading the march with him.

"It is time to stand up and fight back," he warned, *"and the only way to fight back is to support CORE."*

George Raymond also spoke, but instead of his usual warmly mag-netic presence, he stepped up to the lectern with a tone of antagonism and friction in his voice.

"Talk to your ministers about holding meetings in their churches," he said, *"and if they don't, boycott them. Stop giving your money to them. Then they'll come around."*

The attendees of the conference then were divided into two groups. The first group was to continue to work and watch over the develop-ment of the boycott. The second group was to work toward organizing the Madison County Voter Registration Drive. Setting up two groups became strategically successful because it provided a direct form of networking within the Negro community and an all-encompassing interaction.

The "Selective Buying Campaign" that had been used in other boy-cott cities was the one for this group to use to demonstrate to the white business owners the seriousness of equality to all Negros, including their gaining the ability to exercise their right to vote. The campaign would show Canton businesses that there was going to be equal justice for all Negros in Canton. As part of the strategy, the campaign prohibited all Negros from shopping at the boycotted stores or from riding any buses or railways until equal justice was achieved.

One morning soon after the meeting of the National Council of Churches members, Barbara Jean, and I rode to the Freedom House with our mother Susie Brown to meet up with the other members. We were amazed at how many people had turned out there to support the voter registration drive and the boycott. The little "Freedom House" was no longer large enough to accommodate that many people at one time.

When we arrived, we had to sign the sign-in sheet so that the leaders knew everyone who was there in the event that people were taken off to jail. George Raymond suggested pairing us in groups of fifteen march-ers per group, and we left the "House" and went to the Pleasant Green Christ Holiness Church.

When our group of fifteen got there, Charles Morgan, a young white attorney from Birmingham, asked to ride with mother. During the last minute preparations, the group was asked to remove everything from their pockets to avoid any unnecessary arrests by the police. To my sur-prise, there were people who had knives, razors, pistols and other lethal weapons with them. A person within the group held for safekeeping all the collected weapons.

Charles Morgan then informed the other young white marchers in the group that they needed to understand the magnitude of their com-mitment to the civil rights movement.

"*I want to let you know that you are not going on any picnic,*" he told them. "*If you think that you are in Mississippi to change the white man's way of life, you better give up that thought and leave now. If you are not able to accept the name calling -- particularly 'nigger lover' -- you may leave now.*"

After the speech, mother drove Charles Morgan to the courthouse. After sitting quietly for several moments in the front seat of the car, he said to us, "*I hope the police officers think I'm an FBI agent. That may deter some of the problems that could affect the marchers at the courthouse.*"

As we drove around the courthouse, we recognized the faces of ministers from the United Presbyterian Commission on Religion, Race, and the National Council of Churches. They had been part of the organization at the Freedom House. There were also other local ministers there from within the Canton community.

What we hadn't expected, though, was the audacious approach of the white business owners who were now promoting their membership in the White Citizens' Council by flaunting council stickers on the doors and windows of their businesses. Even the banks and the restaurants in town now had them. Later, one supporter of the NAACP reported that the White Citizens' Council president Bobby Yandell had met with the merchants and had told them to keep the Citizens' Council stickers on their businesses at all times to show their commitment to the Citizens' Council.

Finally, the names of all the businesses to be boycotted were made known to the Negros during the next meeting, held at Pleasant Green Christ Hilliness Church.

The list read: To the Negro People of Madison County

The "don't buy" at these stores:

B & B Store
Barq's Bottling Company
C & C Store
Cozy Corner
Florence West Peach Grocery and Markets
Frank Johnson's Grocery
Fred's Dollar Store
J. B. Williamson Grocery
Jingle Jungle
Kerch Credit and Cash Store
Liberty Super Market
Massey's Grocery
May's Food Market
Mosby Drug Store
Noble Drug Store
O. K. Cleaners
Price Lewis Gulf Service Station
Renfroe's Grocery and Market
Salty Sandwich Shop
Stanley's Department Store
T. W. L. Store
Ben Franklin
White Auto Store
A 'Saab Department
Wright Appliance Company

We will not buy at these stores and not buy their products until these stores hire Negro salesclerks.

The salesclerks treat Negro shoppers, especially Negro women courteously.

They desegregate the separate and unequal facilities.

We will not spend our money where we cannot work and where our wives and daughters are not treated respectfully.

FREEDOM NOW!
Madison County Committee on Selective Buying

The White Citizens Council, at this point, had assured business owners of their responsibility to bring an end to the boycott situation in Canton. However, in the meantime, A. Joseph, a fruits and produce wholesale distributor doing business in Canton, apparently voiced concerns to the council about providing uninterrupted service to his customers. He said, *"I only serve a handful of accounts in Canton, the same ones for the past 20 to 25 years. The downtown merchants, who are affected by the boycott, have never been my customers, I am doing no more or no less with them than I have before the boycott. I will consider any plans involving the wholesalers, which would be practical and effective."* But another wholesaler Pearson, manager of the Pet Mike Company in Jackson reported that his downtown customers had threatened to discontinue their business with him if he did not stop delivering products to the Negro business owners—George Washington and Francis Johnson. He declared,

"The Pet Milk Company cannot refuse sales to any store." Although, *"I have been very concerned about the situation and wanted to come to yawl for any suggestions that you can give." "Do you have any suggestions that might help the merchants and yet not violate the free trade policies of my business?"* The council replied, *"Yes. Stop sending your trucks to Canton thus cutting off all grocery outlets, use the excuse of the existing tense situation, you cannot run the risk of your trucks being damaged or drivers being intimidated."' "This would bring about the purpose of depriving the Negro owned stores of Pet products and at the same time would regain the good will of the white merchants. When the boycott is lifted, you can resume trading with all stores."* Pearson replied, *"What about my house-to-house delivery?"* The council, *"You can continue your house-to-house delivery that wouldn't offend the Canton merchants, but cut off the supply to Negro owned stores because they are helping to perpetuate the boycott."*

To that end, the selective buying campaign committee notified all Negros not to buy Mosby's milk or bread products from Hart's Bakery. Because, if Negros cannot work in their businesses and be treated with respect when they patronized them, then they cannot spend their money in their businesses. Consequently, some businesses on the "do not buy list" were there for particular events that had occurred. For example, May's Supermarket placed on the list because the owner of the business slapped a Negro customer. O.K. Cleaners on the list for refusing to clean a Negro customer's clothes and instead tossing them out onto the street.

James Meredith had arrived in Canton, and he attended and spoke at this meeting.

"*I call for a general boycott of everything possible by all Negros,*" he said. "*A Negro's life is not worth the air it takes to keep it alive in Mississippi. This system, under which we live, must be changed at any cost.*"

During the meeting, the Ministers of the National Council of Churches also wrote a letter to the Sears and Roebuck store doing business in Canton. It had engaged in the same discriminatory practices, and the ministers now informed the management that their store was part of the boycott.

As the meeting ended and people were going off in different directions, the Ku Klux Klan arrived wearing their hoods and capes and they paraded around town to make a point of their support for the rights of the white citizens. Soon violence broke out between the Klansmen and the Negros as the hooded men tried to ensnare the conference's attendees in fistfights.

The police soon arrived, but they only arrested some of the young Negro males. None of the whites who actually caused the problem was taken in.

By this time, it was apparent that the White Citizens' Council has grown tired of Percy Greene. His status as an informant had been compromised, and he no longer served any real purpose to their cause. The NAACP had labeled him an "Uncle Tom" and did not want anything to do with him, ever, and Arrington, the editor of the *Eagle Eye* Newspaper in Chicago and a former employee of Greene, had an even lower view of him and called him "the guard from hell."

"Green does not have to die and go to hell to drink Brimstone," Arrington wrote, *"because the Negros in Mississippi have given him his Brimstone free. The Civil Rights leaders in Mississippi do not want him because of his snake attitude toward the progression of Negro girls and boys. Sweetie Bear…is the Grand Dragon of the International Pigeon Droppers Association. He has wandered into the hearts of the Mississippi white hoodlums for money to help keep the Negro in his place. He always has his hands out, bleeding money from the murdering White Citizens' Council, and boasts about how he helped the white hoodlums in Mississippi try to destroy the NAACP…"*

In the meantime, on a cold winter night that March, at a meeting at the Mount Zion Baptist Church, Mr. George Washington, a local Negro entrepreneur, reported that a police officer in ordinary clothes had approached him and asked him to become an informant.

"They wanted me to attend all the meetings and report my findings to them," Mr. Washington said. *"They also wanted me to stop renting my property to CORE."*

When he refused to work as an informant and continued renting out his houses to the movement, the gasoline company removed their pumps from his store, all grocery deliveries to his store stopped, and he began to receive bomb threats.

At about the same time, all the Negro cabbies who drove in Canton were ordered to stop using their private cars as taxicabs because they did not have the proper permits to be operating as taxis. No one had ever bothered with the permits for them before as they only serviced the Negro community.

Sometimes at night, after the other children had gone to sleep, Barbara Jean would fill me in on all the movement's activities in Canton even though our mother didn't like my being as involved as she and Barbara Jean, because of my age. It seemed that spring, just as the water come close to a boiling point, the tensions between the Negros and whites had reached the pinnacle.

The Negros were growing dog-tired of the unceasing brutality and harassment with no observable security or justice by the local enforcement officials. The NAACP local branch scheduled a meeting at the Mount Zion Baptist Church and over one hundred people showed up. George Raymond, Pastor F. P. Parker from Leland, Mississippi, and the pastor of Mount Zion Baptist Church were the speakers. Raymond started the meeting off by informing people that C. O. Chinn and Thaddeus Hewitt were still in prison, but the selective buying campaign was now active and stronger than ever. He also warned those attending of the consequences of going against their race.

"A young Negro woman," he said, "whose last name is Anderson and is the owner of a hat shop, has allowed herself to be used by the white influences. She has betrayed her own race, who dared only to take a stand for what is right. May God have mercy on her and others like her who would put their foot on a black brother's neck in order to keep the white man slinging his bully-clubs over our heads, pointing his pistols at our noses, and most of all, growing fat on our money. Yes, Chinn and Hewitt are in jail because of this misguided, ignorant, treacherous Negro woman. The police force thinks that Negros are stupid. They think that we will stop our fight because these men are in prison. Instead, the imprisonment of these men has released more anger within the Negro community and more support."

Raymond also encouraged Negros to pay their poll taxes and to stay away from businesses on the "do not buy" list. On the other hand, Reverend Parker then spoke about how it might be possible to end the boycott if the city would hire three Negro policemen and crossing school guards; leaving Raymond to think that Reverend Parker and some of the other ministers wanted to end the boycott and run CORE out of town. He felt that if the white business owners were to work through a compromise with Reverend Parker, then local Negros would be led away from CORE through the churches. Little did Raymond know that Parker had become an informant for the White Citizens Council and was doing whatever he was paid to do, that was to sabotage the development *of the NAACP.*

Raymond sadly said, *"In the last century a slave if he had money could sometimes buy his freedom. Now, however, the situation is reversed. We can help to gain our freedom by not buying. By not buying in downtown merchants and by not buying at stores on the boycott list, we can show the store owners that the Negros do not have to be subject to them to feed, clothe, and house us. We will show them that the Negro is not the white man charge. And, we will show ourselves that we do not have to suffer the disrespect and discourtesy from anyone. The boycott is a weapon to gain not only the respect of the community, but also the self-respect of the Negros."*

While the discussions from the meeting were continuing on inside, the police were on the outside taking down the license plate numbers, and those who continued to come to the meeting were told to go home.

When Barbara Jean and I were about to leave, we were asked to get in the back of a police officer patrol car. Unexpectedly, the officer called our mother. Our mother was well known to the Canton Police and was the only woman I knew who had gone toe-to-toe with Sheriff Billy Noble. The officers knew that too, and they let us go. Our mother knew that the result could have been different for Barbara Jean and me that night if she had not stood up for us on that phone call.

As the violence continued to flare in Mississippi, Senator Ed Henry and Representative Hughes introduced a bill that made it illegal to disseminate selective buying campaigns. They wanted to prevent our pamphlets and other insightful critical propaganda from spreading any further.

The leading white citizens were feeling the pressure of the boycott, and more and more statements were being published in the *Madison County Herald* newspaper every week to ensure Negros that everything to safeguard their choice to shop at any business without threats from these "subversive organizations or individual" was being considered.

The White Citizens' Council desperate to find out exactly who was causing the uprising in the town, and the boycott of certain downtown stores. However, rumors began to spread throughout the Negro community that whites were demanding their informants provide them with the names of particular individuals who were responsible for the boycott.

B. Bell, a teacher from Bolivar County and a friend of Reverend Humes, accepted the white folks call and presented to them the names of three Tougaloo College students: Stephen Rutledge, Dora, and Joyce Lander. He may have mentioned the name of Dave Dennis, who was also involved in organizing the boycott. The only goal for each of these students working for the Canton boycott was only to help make the lives of so many Negros better. It was a pivotal moment for local CORE members to learn that the city officials had the actual names of individuals who were involved in the movement. They already had firsthand experience of the pain that could be handed out by the local sheriffs and police officers. It would not be long before the names of CORE members James Earl Chaney, Andrew Goodman, and Michael Schwerner would be fixed in their minds after the three civil rights workers were murdered by a conspiracy of Neshoba County, Mississippi, sheriffs, KKK, and Citizen's Council members.

The names of those three workers would also become fixed in the minds of the American public because newspapers, TV, and radio stations covered that story in detail, but the names of those other Negros and whites who anonymously suffered the same fate were like unheard cries in the night, heard only in the hearts and minds of their friends and families.

As the boycott continued in Canton, a driver for the Pet Milk Company had become concerned with how the boycott had affected the downtown merchants and, as a result, he stopped delivering any Pet Milk products to the two Negro merchants in town, Washington and Johnson.

When the Negro merchants called the company, the driver told them, "*Due to the existing tense situation, I can no longer run the risk of me and my truck being intimidated or hurt.*" He believed that this action would force the Negros to end the boycott and everyone could resume business as usual. Afterward, A. Joseph, Cole Bros., and Fox, a wholesale distributor of fruits, produce and groceries stopped their deliveries to the Negro stores.

Governor Johnson of Mississippi, who had been trying everything possible to end the boycott, then published a statement saying, "*Outside agitators have no rights to be in Mississippi and should attend to their own business where they live. These people do not have the well-being of Mississippi's Negros. If so, they would not have created the racial tensions and bitter feelings in a city like Canton, where the city people long ago provided them with an excellent Y.M.C. A., a swimming pool and playground area superior to the facilities of the white community. Before the agitators came to Canton, Negros were used in businesses, industries, education, and recreation. It is the Canton citizens' interest to end the boycott and restore the harmonious relationship with the Negros they have always enjoyed. The benefits that the Negro has received over the years have come from the whites and not the agitators.*"

The governor's statement did nothing to deter the actions of Negros in the state because Negros was tired of white folks thinking that their survival depended on them. They [Negros] knew that racism was the problem and who it was behind the racism.

As the boycott continued in full force, many whites lost their businesses. Senator Eastland then introduced the "Riot, Boycott Curbs" Bill that aimed to curb civil rights demonstrations and boycotts and the attendant violence. It made boycotts a crime and placed stringent control on civil rights demonstrations.

Senator Eastland wrote, *"It is time we curb the recklessness of these so-called civil rights demonstrations and pass laws to protect the civil rights of the peaceful citizens they hurt. These anti-boycott amendments are needed because these organizations are now threatening community after community with mass mob action and economic reprisal if their arbitrary demands are not met."*

Many of the participants in the boycott, in Canton, were Negro children. They picketed the businesses after school and on weekends and carrying signs calling for an end to the injustice. The signs read, "Stop the Killing," "End Police Brutality," "Civil Rights, Now or Civil Strife," "Jobs, Freedom, Now," and "Vote for Justice, Now."

In a somewhat desperate challenge to control the boycott, some merchants jump-started a campaign, based on Senator Ed Henry's idea, to discourage Negros from boycotting their businesses by taking photos of them demonstrating in front of their stores. Perhaps this measure was made in an attempt to deter or frighten the Negros, but the tactic did not work.

The merchants then created a "gimpy," a phony trick of some sort, whereby manufacturers would pay their Negro workers one-half of their pay in cash or checks and the other half in species. Because of the tremendous buying power of the many Negros used at the production plants in

Canton, the merchants needed to succeed in getting the Negros back into the habit of trading in downtown Canton, regardless of the ongoing determination of boycott leaders.

The production plants would pay their Negro workers fifty percent in cash or checks. The remaining fifty percent of their pay was paid with imprinted species for a particular store. All species had the printed words, *"This note is worth $ _____ when properly endorsed and presented for cashing at any of the following stores."* Then the list of stores was printed on the species.

The Negros couldn't just go to that store, cash the species, take the money, and spend it somewhere else. To make the gimpy payoff, the Negro had to go to the store with the imprinted merchant and make purchases there in order to use the species. This was the white factory owners' shrewd attempt at getting the Negros back into those stores on the "do not buy" list to spend money.

At the same time, local merchants created the *"Cash your Payroll Check and Win a Prize"* gimpy to engage the Negro's buying power. When the Negros went to the store to cash their checks, the merchants gave them a ticket with numbers printed on them, and the Negros would place their tickets into a box. Once a week on the courthouse square, a drawing, was held, and the holder of the lucky number got a cash prize of $50.00. When the winner got his or her "prize"; however, he or she could only receive the prize in the form of a species.

If a Negro refused to receive the fifty percent cash or check and species payout, he or she lost their job.

Nevertheless, their plans did not work. At the Asbury Baptist Church meeting called by the branch president, discussion pertaining to the merchants' new prevue of tricks to get the working Negros back in their stores was heavily debated.

In the middle of the meeting, the informant Walden Paden stood up and asked, *"What would it take for the boycott to end in Canton, and what if the white community exercised payback against the Negros for the boycott?"*

"Not one thing," was the answer from the rest of the crowd.

At the meeting, discussion of how the people would celebrate Easter. It was decided that none of the Negros would buy Easter outfits or material to make them from those businesses whose names were on the "do not buy" list. Instead, we'd all celebrate Easter in old clothes.

This strategy proved successful because some stores went out of business. However, the owner of the May's Grocery Market went to Medger Evers, the NAACP Field Secretary, and asked him to entreat the Negros to stop boycotting his store because he was losing a lot of customers, and his business could not remain open without the Negro customers.

Medger Evers was not the least bit moved, and he told everyone to continue with the boycotting as usual.

The NAACP leaders thought it was time to set the integration talks into action, and they speculated about what business might be the first to try to integrate. Some suggested the movie theatre, while others suggested one or the other of the cafes. The decision was made to take on one white eatery establishment first and then the Bill Will Motel and the Greyhound bus company after.

The NAACP field leader Medger Evers knew that this would prove different from the boycott and would be much more dangerous because the Negros were about to embark into territory that was forbidden to them and was strictly reserved for white folks. We all accepted the challenge, though, and moved toward the task of integration.

From that point, on, the police brutality began to run out of control. Those hired to protect and serve became lawless. Violence and terror ensued and hassling or killing a Negro for doing nothing seemed to become the standard.

Young Negro males and females who wanted the right to sit down at Wardell's and Mecca Cafes for dinner were refused service, spit on, and yelled at with vulgarities and racial slurs. Other students, in groups of ten, went to check in at the Bill Will Motel, but they were not allowed to. Instead, they found themselves in the middle of a large crowd of whites in front of the motel with sticks, bats, pipes, and knives. When the police arrived, the sheriff spoke to the white crowd alone.

"Leave and don't let this happen again," Sheriff Noble told them quietly. *"Do you want to get yourselves in trouble by molesting these organizations trying to integrate these areas of businesses? If you do, we will not take part in it."*

The mob left.

The Ministerial Alliance group then tried to talk to Sheriff Noble, but only received threats in return.

"I can take five dollars, a half-pint of whiskey, and a nigger," he told them, *"and have all you outsiders killed before I see integration in Canton. It will be over my dead body."*

One of the ministers asked Noble why Negros could not vote.

"There are two thousand white registered voters and two hundred-fifty nigger registered voters in Canton," Noble told him, *"and if we let all the niggers vote, it would be like a leak in a dam and a little while the niggers would run Canton."*

The sheriff's deputy then chimed in, *"Negros will never integrate or vote in a block anyway because they are too suspicious of each other."*

In the meantime, the Ku Klux Klan were increasing their presence in Canton. It felt like the gates of hell had opened wider than usual to allow these vicious men loose on the Negro people. Retaliation against Negros was their main objective. They opposed the civil rights movement, everything associated with the NAACP, and their plan was to preserve segregation by any means necessary.

With the Klan's greater presence, bombings of churches increased. Lynching's and beatings were on the rise, and other barbarous attacks took more Negro lives. Burned crosses on the front lawns of many Negro's homes and more church burnings became the pattern. Like monsters in the night, the KKK paraded around in ghostly sheets, but we knew that only cowards hide their faces.

On June 12, 1963, the *Clarion Ledger* newspaper reported that Medgar Evers, the NAACP Field Secretary, was gunned down by Byron De La Beckwith, a segregationist who was born in Colusa, California, and was known for his outspoken views against integration. It became a quiet time as Negros mourned the loss of this courageous young man; a young man shot down by one white coward in the night.

Barbara Jean had become even more active in the Civil Rights movement, and she didn't realize what might lie in her future result just a year down the road. Mother had talked to her often about not putting her life on the line. At this point, in the movement, things were changing, and that meant danger with her marching and situated visibly in the boycott and voter registration drives.

After the death of Medgar Evers, mother told Barbara Jean that it would be a good idea for her not to continue her involvement in the movement. Barbara Jean was a young, headstrong girl who believed in what she was doing, and though she quietly listened to her mother, she did not stop working as a volunteer in the movement. She canvassed neighborhoods and distributed voter registration leaflets, and she announced to as many Negros as she could the dates and times of scheduled workshops conducted by the COFO staff throughout the county.

CHAPTER SIX

Voter Registration and Freedom Summer: The Genesis of Lights

The boycott was efficient.

On January 13, 1964, Senator Ed Henry met with the Canton Merchants because the Mississippi Sovereignty Commission had proposed that Canton's white citizens place an ad in the *Madison Herald* again to show their support for and protection of any Negro, who wanted to do business in white stores.

Nevertheless, a week later, the Pleasant Green Holiness Church was packed with both Negros and whites. There were over thirty-two familiar faces in the crowd as well as many who had never been there before. Charles Evers started the meeting by telling the people how successful the boycott and integration had been, and he urged them to continue to stay away from those businesses who did not hire Negros.

He then passed out as a reminder a piece of paper that read:

NEGRO SHOPPERS!

The Boycott Goes On Until We Win
Equality in Job Hiring and Promotion
End of Segregated Drinking Fountains-Seating – Restroom
Use of Courtesy Titles: "Miss, Mrs., and Mr.
Service on First-Come, A First-Serve basis

*"Don't Buy in Any Downtown Stores. Don't Buy
in Jackson on Capital Street, Either."*

"Mississippi Negros could revolt," Claude Weaver, one of the men who
had been sitting quietly in the audience, said, *"and the fight for Negro
rights is not a question of a little unpleasantness, but a question of the right
to vote. Negros in Mississippi don't even have the right to say they don't have
any rights. If you're a Negro in Mississippi and a white man comes up to you
and says 'Boy, are you happy?' you better say, 'Yeah, cause if you don't, you
goanna be dead or at least bruised."*

After the meeting had ended, the police did not arrest anyone, as
they had often before, but they did take down license plate numbers.

On January 21, the Canton Board of Aldermen passed an ordinance
prohibiting the distribution of pamphlets in the city without a permit
from the Mayor or the Chief of Police and the next day the *Madison
County Herald* published the law:

*"It is forbidden to circulate and distribute handbills, circular posters,
or pamphlets on any sidewalk, metropolitan streets, or in any public places
within the city of Canton."*

Regardless of the new law, Barbara Jean was not about to stop from
participating in the boycott or passing out information pertaining to the boy-
cotted stores. She knew it had become her responsibility to make sure that the
Negro community was aware of those stores on the "do not buy" list.

The Negros of Madison County knew that voter registration was
the ultimate dare to the white community, and a great deal of pressure
had been placed on the shoulders of the Negros, as Canton became an
increasingly violent arena. The disturbances continued as Negros continued to exercise their rights to vote.

Civil rights activists from out of town continued to arrive to help the
Negros prepare for the biggest dare of all—*Freedom Day.* Some of them
stayed at the Freedom House and some stayed with Susie Brown. The

name Freedom Day had been chosen because it was a day that would encourage all eligible Negros to register to vote.

At 7:00 p.m., Tuesday, February 22, James Collier of CORE called a meeting at the Pleasant Green Christ Holiness Church to discuss the line of defense for the voter registration drive and for the selection of candidates to challenge Eastland and Stennis for the United State Senate races. Many names were tossed back and forth until the group selected Chamberlain of Hattiesburg and Houston of Vicksburg to run. They also discussed adding Medgar Evers' widow to the list of candidates for the United States Congress, as well as Annie Devine.

As the crowd in the church grew more and more excited, Collier assured them that there would be strong Negro support for these candidates.

"After all," he said, *"this is the purpose of organizing the freedom schools in Mississippi. To teach the Negros how to register and vote."*

In the meantime, as George Washington, a local Negro grocery and property owner, sat quietly in the meeting finally stood up and spoke about the incidents that had taken place at his business earlier that day. George Washington was in his middle fifties and a lifelong resident of Canton. He reported that he was arrested for burning trash without a permit in front of his business even though he has burned trash so many times before without any problem. Dennis and Farmer quickly realized that the boycott was working. They [Dennis and Farmer] told the group that Barq's Bottling Company and Gordon's Jewelers had revised their hiring practices to hire Negros and had improved their customer relations with their Negro customers. Since Barq's Bottling Company and Gordon's jewelers had complied with the listed suggestion, Denis and James suggested removing them from the "do not buy" list. Reverend Parker of Mount Zion Baptist Church wanted to go even further and end the boycott altogether.

"*If the City hires school crossing guards for the Negro community and Negro police officers,*" he proposed, "*the boycott should be lifted.*"

Charles Evers said the boycott should only be lifted after there was federalized desegregation in Mississippi. All the others agreed.

Crane, a troubleshooter for CORE, emphasized the security measures for the people participating in the freedom day protest march from the church to the downtown courthouse. The other CORE members, C. O. Chinn, George Raymond, and James Collier were now out of prison, and they were helping organize the protest to the courthouse.

McCain, a young man in his twenties with a small mustache and a troubleshooter for CORE, then posed a question, "*How are we going to get such a large number of Negros to the next scheduled meeting to march to the courthouse?*"

Two other men, Robert, a young man in his twenties, and Bill, in his thirties with thinning brown hair, recommended using the CORE station wagons to pick up as many Negros as possible. All agreed. Reverend McCloud then asked James Collier to contact the schools' principals and get their support for "Freedom Day" by declaring a holiday so that students could participate in the protest.

On February 23, at the Saint Paul Baptist Church meeting was called in order to finalize the plans for the Freedom Day. B. L. Cox of North Carolina, a man in his thirties with brown skin and dark curly hair, was the speaker.

"*I will lead the march to the courthouse,*" he said. "*I want you to tell your friends and families about the march and let them know there will be a host of out-of-town CORE members to march with them. If there should be a trouble break out, we'll all be here to protect you. We are not afraid.*"

Another speaker, Jerome Smith, also spoke to the audience to encourage them.

"I am one of the first Freedom Riders in Jackson," he said, introducing himself, *"and I've been in and out of prison and I am not afraid to go back. The white segregationists killed Medgar Evers. Do not let his death be in vain. Tell every girl, boy, man and woman to stay out of school Friday and let us make that day a legal holiday."*

Concerned about the upcoming Freedom Day, Governor Ross Barnet signed the Mutual Assistance Pacts Bill on February 25th. The Bill gave officials the right for one municipality to lend law enforcement to another in connection with Civil Rights Movement activities. No one knew what was about to happen in Canton on Freedom Day Friday, February 28th. Not even the Negros.

Thursday, February 27th, was a cold and rainy night, but Negros came in droves to the last meeting before the Freedom Day. They were to finalize all activities for that day, including how they would march from the church to the courthouse. James Collier showed everyone how to fill out the Voter Registration Form and encouraged them not to be intimidated, no matter what happened while they were completing the form at the courthouse.

Meanwhile, to show solidarity against Freedom Day, the white citizens prominently displayed their White Citizens' Council stickers on the doors of their businesses. The Jackson, Mississippi, KKK had arrived. They came to Canton to help the members of the Citizens' Council of Madison County prepare against the Negros march on Freedom Day. The FBI had also arrived in Canton. They were easily recognizable. Because of their black or blue suits and polished shoes.

The atmosphere in Canton was still one of tension, but also, for the Negros, one of excitement, too.

On the day before Freedom Day, two ministers, Reverend Norman Simmons and Reverend Joseph Atkins reportedly wandered into Foote Campbell's office.

While standing in that place, softly, they asked Campbell, *"Can we stay here to observe the voting activities?"*

"No," Campbell answered, *"but you can go across the square and watch from the Noble Insurance Company."*

Then Claude Sutton, a reporter, entered Campbell's office while the ministers were still there.

"Can you tell me how many Negros have registered to vote, and how many have failed the Literacy Exam?" he asked.

Campbell would not answer.

On the frigid February morning of February 28th, Freedom Day, over one hundred Negros and whites marched from the Freedom House to the county courthouse. There were fifteen Ministers with them from various denominations of the National Council of Churches of New York, Cincinnati, Indianapolis, Hays and Wichita Kansas, Chicago, Illinois, Chapel Hill, North Carolina, and even Westfield, New Jersey. They came in cars, on foot and in mule-drawn wagons to form one of the largest voting-rights demonstrations ever in Canton.

The marchers were harassed and threatened along the way by law enforcement officers fortified with shotguns and tear gas and by the KKK. As the Negros walked to the courthouse to register to vote, one elderly woman said to the officers, *"I am too old for junk. We do not want any trouble. All we want is to become citizens like everybody else."*

Many Negro students from Rogers High and Holy Child Missionary School, including other Negro schools, walked out to recognize and join the marchers. Unbeknownst to local officials, Negro parents had kept their sons and daughter's home to show their support for the Freedom Day.

For hours, Negro students from Rogers, Camden and the Flora schools, as well as people from Sharon, Pickens, Farmhaven, and Camden, waited in lines in the frigid weather outside the courthouse to take the Voters' Literacy exam.

Campbell would only allow a few in at a time to take the literacy exam, and more and more lined up to wait outside the courthouse for their turn. All day long, the armed law enforcement authorities questioned each Negro in line about where they lived. Some were removed from the line, including Charles Evers, because they did not live in Madison County. The National Council of Churches stood across the square observing the voter activities from afar while the out of town law enforcement officers stood right on the street. It looked like the Mutual Assistance Pacts Bill was an apparent success based on the number of officers that had surrounded Canton.

"Every city, large, and small is standing by to help Canton," the Sheriff said, obviously happy to have the help.

There were deputies standing all around the courthouse who shouted on and off to a large crowd to get off the sidewalks and not to block the streets. The crowd adhered to the officers' warnings because nobody wanted to do anything that would cause trouble or jeopardize their mission to vote.

There were no white people in the registration lines, but there were white photographers on the square by the courthouse, and they wouldn't move away when the officers yelled.

The superintendent of public schools, Robert Cox, was walking up and down the lines checking to see if any of his teachers was trying to register. Apparently, a teacher who was not connected with the NAACP or the voter drive was there to transfer his voting precinct from one county to Madison when Cox approached him.

Cox reportedly suggested to the teacher,

"It is not a good idea for you to move your voting rights now because it would be a bit of trouble to make the transfer." He then asked the teacher, *"Do you see any children in this voting line whose parents live somewhere else?"*

Unwillingly, the teacher replied.

"I see some students whose parents live in other districts like Chicago and Detroit," he said, *"but a few that I see do not know where their parents live."*

The leaders told the students not to skip school, but only some did return to their classes.

When the drive ended in mid-afternoon, only four Negros had been able to take the literacy test required to qualify as registered voters. Normally, it took thirty days to know if one had passed or failed the test, but things were different today.

"No one passed," Campbell, announced to the crowd.

Shortly before the voter's registration drive ended, George Raymond of CORE had spoken to the news media.

"Today's activities disprove previous statements made by local and state officials that a large assembly of Negros would cause violence," he announced. *"The drive showed that Negro people and civil rights organizations are capable of maintaining order."*

CORE representative David Dennis also made a statement.

"We are trying this mad effort because the people have to do something to combat the tremendous pressure that they have to go against."

The next day, Saturday, February 29th, twenty Negros were in line on the west side of the courthouse to take the Literacy Exam. Later, as Campbell closed his office, he informed the Negros that no one passed and then he pushed them out to close his office.

On Monday, March 2nd, more Negros gathered to take the Literacy exam. Ida Barnes had started her exam that Saturday but did not finish. She was allowed to come back Monday to complete the exam, but she, too, was later informed that she did not pass.

The NAACP began to notice trends in the number of Negros failing the exam, contacted the Justice Department, and then, on behalf of three hundred Negros, filed affidavits of discrimination with the Justice Department in Washington, DC. Soon after the discrimination suit had been filed, Mr. Moore of the Justice Department arrived at Foote Campbell's office. He asked Campbell to show him the records of those people who had registered as well as the ones who had attempted to register, but had failed.

"I have only registered those who qualified, and I will not be compromised by registering anyone who is not qualified," Campbell told him.

March 7, George Raymond sent a signed statement to United States Senators James O. Eastland and John C. Stennis with one hundred eighty-three signatures requesting the passing of the Civil Rights Bill of 1963-1964. Barbara Jean, as well as mother, had signed the requested declaration.

Senator Ed Henry immediately let it be known that pamphlets would be distributed to the entire house to prohibit the bill from passing.

As a result of the Canton Freedom Day's success, many of the local students traveled to Greenwood to support the Greenwood students' Freedom Day. They left Canton in a private bus owned by a local Negro man, and soon many law enforcement officers were following them. When the bus reached the Greenwood city limits, Deputy Noble from Madison County and some other officials from Greenwood stopped the bus. The driver was given a ticket for an improper license tag. He was also cited for driving a school bus of the wrong color; even though, his bus was the official yellow appearance as it was for all school buses.

The students were then removed from the bus. Still, decided to support the Greenwood Freedom Day, they walked from the station to meet up with the local students at the county courthouse. At the end of the day's freedom activities, the Canton students were ready to leave, but they couldn't because their bus situation had not been resolved. Many local Good Samaritan truck drivers provided them, with rides home.

The students made it home and were able to place the trip behind them as they concentrated on preparations for the next scheduled Freedom Day for Canton.

However, their parents were less forgiving of the action perpetrated by law enforcement. They wrote a letter to the school board, which read, *"We, the parents of Rogers High youth, protest the presence and harassment by the police on and around the campus during school. There had been no disturbance, violence, or disobedience on the part of the student body to merit such sudden attention by the police. The only unlawful act committed by anyone was the incident when hundreds of children were turned away from school by the school officials. Instead of placing police to patrol the school, we request the police department furnish patrolmen at the street crossings instead."*

Canton students continued the voter registration drive. There were reporters in Canton to cover all of the activities. There were law enforcement officers from every county in the town. There were men armed with weapons strategically positioned at a number of locations near the courthouse. The KKK presence was evident, as well. It was an epic time for this little country town.

On March 26th, Mississippi State Senator Ed Henry, in an effort to get the boycott lifted proposed two approaches to the city officials. He recommended that the City Council announce in the *Madison County Herald* that they had been considering hiring a part-time Negro Crossing Guard to work in the area of the Negro school and that the City Council was taking applications to hire at least one Negro for the job. In addition, Henry suggested that all merchants remove the Citizens' Council stickers from their storefronts because these stickers, regardless of the unity and policies they represented, were actually a deterrent to the Negro trade.

Senator Henry's proposal was one more desperate attempt to end the boycott, but it did not work.

During the month of April, the voter registration drive was still in development, due in large measure to the efforts of C. O. Chinn, and large numbers of Negros gathered to march to the courthouse from Canton, Camden, Pickens, Sharon and Farmhaven to take the literacy exam. Campbell would still only allow four to five in at one time, though, and the FBI was still active in the county investigating the local police department's intimidation of Negros when they tried to register to vote. The do-not-buy boycott remained extremely effective, and it appeared that it would be quite some time before the situation returned to normal in the county.

During the first two weeks of May; however, there were eighteen Negros at the courthouse trying to register. As of Mother's Day, the boycott of businesses was still going strong, and there were almost no Negros patronizing businesses with citizens' council stickers on the doors.

Bill Majors, the manager of Fred's Dollar Store, allegedly asked permission from the White Citizens' Council to remove the sticker from his store door because it might bring Negros into his store to shop for Mother's Day.

After a successful Mother's Day boycott, James Collier called a meeting for as many Negros as were able to attend the meeting on short notice. He advised the group that he was putting a fundraiser together on May 23rd to raise money for the activities and workers during the second Freedom Day activities.

On a beautiful spring day, May 29th, the second Freedom Day in Canton, a large number of Negros marched from the Mount Zion Baptist Church to the downtown courthouse.

SNCC leader Farmer addressed the crowd on the way and encouraged them about the plan, saying, *"There must be a good show of patronage from all our people,"* he said, *"in order to reach the goals that have been set for this extraordinary time. We need the publicity to support our goal of a decent education, jobs, and homes. We have waited too long for men to give us these things, but they will never give us a thing. We must fight for our freedom, not with violence, but lawfully, through the ballot. We can have what we desire if we are willing to step forward and become registered voters. The world is watching the South. The world is watching us."*

As a large group reached the courthouse, they were turned back. McKinley, a Negro man in his twenties, was struck several times in the head with nightsticks by three officers. He was taken to the King's Daughter Hospital and then afterwards, jailed.

More Negros were jailed that day, too, even Barbara Jean. At noon, fourteen more Negros and whites marched from the Mount Zion Baptist Church to the Madison County Courthouse. They were arrested for marching without a permit. Around 1:00 p.m., a group of thirteen Negros marched from the church to the courthouse, and they too were arrested.

The Mississippi Highway Patrol had arrived in Canton, armed with shotguns, rifles, and pistols, to support the local officers and police units.

The marchers never backed down. At 2:00 p.m., a group of nineteen Negros marched to the courthouse, and they were arrested, as well. Then five out-of-state whites were arrested for marching without permits. Still another group of nine Negros was arrested at 2:30 p.m. for trying to picket the courthouse.

By 3:00 p.m., thirty-five Negros, had taken the voters' registration examination, and twenty-five more were waiting to take the test.

Many Negros and whites were still in prison that Friday night, but three were released because they were juveniles less than fifteen years old, including Barbara Jean. They were released to their parents and told to appear in Juvenile court Monday morning.

There were more Negros in town than usual this Saturday as they were there to take the voting literacy exam. However, the courthouse was closed. The large crowd of Negros was seen as a threat to the Sheriff, so he asked every business that sold food, beer, or liquor to close early that day.

The harassment and violence continued. Lewis, a local white gas station attendant, shot five teens involved in the civil rights movement with a shotgun while they passed by his gas station on Peace Street. They were only walking to one of the local community functions. Although they were not seriously wounded, Lewis was only charged with unlawfully discharging a firearm within the city limits. He paid a $500.00 fine and was free to go.

Pandemonium broke out in the streets of Canton between Negros, whites, and KKK when Negros heard the verdict was to free Lewis with a minimum fine. How could it be possible, they questioned, that Negros lives were worth no more than a few pennies?

Meanwhile, the project leader, Robert (Bob) Moses, twenty-nine, from New York, spoke to the CORE team, *"As you come into Mississippi you bring with you the concerns of the country. The country does not identify with Negros. It identifies with whites. With that interest comes a little more security for you. It is still up for grabs whether that security can be for the Negros of Mississippi."* At that time, a CORE member approach Bob and whisper something in his ear. Bob later looked over the crowd and said, *"Three of our member are lost. They left yesterday going to Philadelphia, Mississippi. No one there has heard from them."* Those workers were Chaney, Goodman, and Schwerner. These young men established the CORE Freedom School at the Mount Nebo Methodist Church in Philadelphia. A school to help Negros achieve social and economic equality in Neshoba County. However, that weekend they left the Canton Freedom House for Philadelphia because they had heard about the Mount Nebo Church burning. As a result of their going back to Neshoba County, they went missing.

The leaders of the local NAACP chapter were determined to find out what had happened to these young men, and they traveled to Philadelphia. When they arrived at the courthouse there, the officials would not allow them to go to the site of the burned church.

As the report rose back and forth between the town's officials and the NAACP members, a large crowd of white men gathered outside the Philadelphia courthouse. The leaders of the white group began insulting the Negros, calling them "niggers" and yelling at them that they had no right to be in their town.

At one point, the leader of the whites addressed the NAACP attorney by his first name.

"Only my friends and associates have permission to call me by my first name."

"Now you are here," the white man told him, "and you will do things our way, and I will call you what I want."

"If that is the way you want to play it," the NAACP attorney replied, "then that is the way it will be."

Charles, another NAACP member, interrupted the rising tempers of the two and asked, "Are there any Negros voting in Neshoba County?"

"Now, Charles, you know damn well niggers cannot vote here," the town's white leader said.

Someone in the background yelled out to stop the name-calling.

The leader continued with his rant, though.

"What are you if you ain't niggers?" he said. "There are only three kinds of people, whites, faggots, and niggers."

"Yeah?" said the NAACP attorney. "What if I called you a cracker or poor white trash?"

By this time, a large crowd of white men had surrounded the NAACP members' cars. The NAACP members started to leave the courthouse.

Deputy Sheriff Price then pushed his way through the crowd and yelled at the NAACP members, *"Get out of town! Get going! Get out of town now!"*

As they were leaving one NAACP man said, *"We could have been killed."*

The members returned to Canton to meet with the CORE workers at their headquarters. By then the members of CORE had heard that the bodies of their missing colleagues had been found, beaten, shot, and mutilated. It was a sad time.

The NAACP leader planned a meeting at the Asbury Methodist Church to re-engage the people and refocus attention on the Canton boycott and voter registration.

When we arrived there, a young white man dressed in a Highway Patrol Officer Uniform stood out front and yelled, *"I am going to kill me a nigger tonight."*

After another similar incident with Sheriff Noble, the National Council of Churches wrote a letter to Mayor L. S. Matthew:

"We protest the conduct of the police department. We do not like the impertinence, aggressive handling, and vexation of the people. We disapprove of your interference in our orderly meetings and marches. We were on the sidewalk when Sheriff Noble used uncouth and vulgar language. Those austere words were not needed because we did nothing wrong. We protest the bullying of people attempting to register too. We should not have been asked to give our names to the police. We want a meeting with you to discuss ways to prevent these things in the future."

The Mayor would not meet with the group.

"I will not meet with niggers," he said. *"I run this city. They don't."*

The actions of the Canton mayor, police officers, and sheriff's deputies continued to be embedded with hatred and bigotry. Violence was an everyday occurrence.

An emergency meeting was then called at the Liberty Missionary Baptist Church. The church was filled to capacity. Police officers were on the outside taking down license plate numbers, shining flashlights into the church windows, buzzing their sirens, making loud noises, and taking photos. Many inside were afraid because they knew of the brutality throughout the county at the hands of the police.

Intimidation and violence increased. Faced with a selective buying campaign, school integration and now the voter registration drive, the white community retaliated. They drove through Negro communities and yelled threats of killing anyone who tried to registrar to vote. Twice more the police raided the Freedom House, where the CORE team still lived. One night George Raymond, the CORE Task Force worker, was told to get out of town, but he would not leave.

Later that night, Essie Louise Bridgeman, a Negro CORE worker, reported to police that someone had called and said, *"The Freedom House will be burned out tonight."* Elaine Weinberger, a White CORE worker, also reported receiving a call saying, *"The Freedom House will be bombed at midnight."* The caller identified himself as a member of the KKK.

John Newman of CORE reported the calls to the Justice Department in Washington, DC, and to the FBI. No one ever heard of any result from the complaints.

The boycott was now going into its second year; it had become even more effective and stronger; in fact, the selective buy campaign was so effective that one reporter from the *Mississippi Free Press* wrote, *"The toll in the selective buying campaign is beginning to mount. As the boycott continues to bear down, more and more stores are falling victims from the attack of dollar warfare. Stores which used to treat Negro customers with discourtesy and get away with it are not getting away with it anymore."* Desperately, the merchants wanted nothing more than to end the boycott. But, not the Negros as they continued to apply the pressure on the white businesses. For the July 4th holiday, for example, Canton Negros bought their holiday supplies from George Washington's grocery store or killed their pigs and chickens to keep from buying at the white boy-cotted stores. At the same time, seven additional CORE workers had arrived in Canton, Reverend Edward Maury, Reverend A. Saloff, Farley Wheelwright, Julius Belser, Rims Barber, Richard Milford, Boardmon Kathan, and George Coleman. These men were from as far away as New York, Illinois, Michigan, and Minnesota, and had come to Canton to help with the school integration.

By September 4th, the start of the school year, integration was final-ly completely out in the open, but even more violence erupted thanks to the KKK. Nineteen Negro children applied for transfers to the all-white Canton High School. Eighteen of them traveled in automobiles while one walked to the school. Including Barbara Jean. The integration was well organized because ministers from out of town worked diligently preparing the Negro students for that time.

The students' ages ranged from twelve to eighteen and George Raymond, and Dave Dennis accompanied them to the White school. The Negro students were asked several questions by the school officials, and then they were permitted to fill out applications for transfer. As they completed the application, they were asked again, why they wanted to transfer.

"I want to transfer," Barbara Jean spoke out, "because the Negro schools do not teach foreign languages, do not have science laboratories, physical edu-cation classes, and they do not have good libraries."

All of the students was given a note to take to their parents.

The note read, "The request for transfer is being studied. We are re-questing parents to send the students to the schools where they were registered until further notice."

"We will all be back next week for classes," George Raymond told the school officials.

That next week, when the students arrived back on the school grounds, they encountered armed law enforcement offers commanded by Sheriff Billy Noble. They refused to allow the students in the school. Parents were forced to take their children back home or back to their individual schools.

That night George Washington's store was bombed for the second time. The explosive device destroyed the west side of the building, blowing out windows, doors and the concrete sidewalk. The explosion caused a ripple effect and shock waves were felt for several blocks. No one doubted that the bomb was in direct retaliation for the attempted school integration earlier that day.

On September 8th, thirteen of the original nineteen Negro high school students returned to the Canton High School, and all thirteen elementary school students returned to the Canton Elementary School. This time the parents and the NAACP were more prepared. The Negro students and their parents came by the carload. A black station wagon, a white and red station wagon and a 1957 two-tone Buick drove up, guarded by armed federal troops. Sheriff Noble was waiting for them.

The federal troops did not deter Sheriff Noble from intimating two of the Negro parents, though, Luella Chambers and Hattie Mae Oliver.

"You Negro girls," Noble said to the two mothers, *"need to keep your children in the Negro schools. The white folk here don't want your kind in their school."*

Two months later, around the Thanksgiving break, some students at Rogers High walked out of school because Mosby's milk was still being served in the cafeteria. Mosby's was on the "do not buy" list. The parents of those students also voiced their disappointment with Principal Jones for allowing the milk company to continue delivering their product to the school when the principal knew the company was on the boycott list.

The principal called an emergency meeting of the students' parents, and the Superintendent of Education Allen stood up to speak to them.

"Those students who walked out of school are hurting themselves, their parents and their teachers," he said. *"The ones who stayed got a full day of learning. Those who walked out learned nothing. They will receive a zero if they are not able to present a written reason to the office for being absent. Now ask whom being out of school offended... No one is going to force your children to come to school, but those students who come to school and then leave are subject to suspension."*

The parents were angry and were not about to be bullied by the Department of Education. They walked out. Later, the parents called an emergency meeting of their own and invited Charles Evers to be the speakers. When Principal Jones heard about the meeting, he asked the superintendent to attend. However, when C. O. Chinn arrived, he was arrested and charged with a concealed weapon violation and trespassing earlier on school property.

Charles Evers spoke to the overcrowded church filled with both Negros and Whites about the importance of unity and registering to vote.

"Why do we do it?" Evers asked the public. *"We do it because voting is the basic right of a citizen in a democracy, and we want to have this right. It is wrong not to try. We do it even though we may lose our jobs or suffer harassment. We do it because we know we can only change government if we vote for the men who run it. We must vote! We will vote! We need to show strong support for the Canton boycott. Do not buy on Capital Street in Jackson, either."*

He also spoke against the police brutality at the hand of Sheriff Noble and his officers when the Negros had tried to register to vote earlier during the week. He called Sheriff Noble *"The bully of Madison County."*

In spite of that, while the meeting was taking place inside the church, the law enforcement officers were busy outside recording license plate numbers. The police learned from one of those license numbers that a car at the meeting was registered to Mr. Mansell, a prominent white citizen of Camden. It was suspected that his Negro driver used the car to transport Negros to the meeting, and it was believed, too, that the car was used without Mansell's permission.

Instead of arresting the driver, the officers monitored the movement of the car carrying Negros to NAACP meetings. Finally, at the end of one night's meeting after the driver dropped off his last Negro passenger, he was arrested for auto theft.

In next to no time, there was one more church burning this time in the Gluckstadt community of Canton. It was burned down in the middle of the night. As there had been so many church burnings because of the school integration activities, a Quaker group representing the Committee of the Concerned from Pennsylvania, Connecticut and California came to Canton to investigate the burnings and to help in the rebuilding process of the churches.

In December, workers from the Council of Federated Organizations, a coalition of the major civil rights movements in Mississippi, had arranged for Negros to meet at the Freedom House early in the morning of December 3rd to board transportation from the Freedom House to the polling precincts. Local officials heard that the COFO workers were going to be using some form of transportation to transport Negros to the polling places, and they sent deputies to investigate. The city and school officials believed that the school buses would be used as a mode of transportation. Claude Moore, a candidate for the Agricultural Stabilization Conservation Board Community Committee, transported as many Negros who could fit in his automobile and other COFO workers used their own vehicles to transport the rest of the Negros to the voting precincts. One more showdown was prevented.

The COFO workers had positioned themselves at each polling precinct for the upcoming vote of Negro candidates. The workers were equipped with walkie-talkie radios, and there were both whites and Negros workers at the polls to support the Negro voters. That day, Negros ended up voting for the white candidates and one Negro candidate because the names of all the other Negros, who should have been on the ballot had been left off.

The election had been for members of the Agricultural Stabilization Conservation Board. These were elected positions that oversaw the pasture improvements program, the cotton control program, the feed and grain program, the farm storage facilities program, the conservation reserve program, the wool program, and the attendant domestic cotton program price support (for cotton or crop loans). To qualify for the elected position, the candidate had to be a farmer, reside on a farm, be twenty-one, be a landowner, or be an operator, a tenant, or a sharecropper.

The chair of the ASC committee was important because this committee directed the program for all farmers for twelve months. To deter the efforts of Negros to run the ASC programs, white citizens changed the rules before the election and changed the status of sharecroppers to that of wage-hands. That way they would not be qualified to vote in the election.

CHAPTER SEVEN

We Shall Not be Moved

January 1965. There had not been much excitement in town as it had been previous. On the other hand, there were civil rights workers and attorneys there gathering information regarding the discrimination suit filed by the NAACP against the city and county for misconduct during the ASC election and the Mississippi Freedom Democratic Party. As the subpoenas dispensed, the Negros affected by the situation were also required to give depositions about the discriminatory practice imposed against them by the circuit's clerk.

It almost seemed calm on the streets of Canton, but the, underlying tension had hardly ceased to exist. This quietness only meant that Judge Hendrix's court was in session.

Meanwhile, George Raymond left a community meeting and drove north towards Highway 51.

Later the next day, Raymond reported, *"cars of policemen stopped, moved me from the car and led me behind a patrolman's car where I was challenged to a fistfight. The constable removed his badge, gun, and watch, and then verbally ridiculed me to get me to fight. I remained quiet, and the constable kicked me several times, knocking me against the back of several police cars."*

Conversely, the person in the car with Raymond was not able to see anything and, therefore, could not help his friend. Though, he tried several times to open the door but the policemen would always block him in. Weighing it all in, the only other witnesses were the policemen themselves, and they were not talking.

They did have something to say to Raymond though.

"Every time the Justice Department comes to Canton it will cost the Negro community big time," one officer told him as he walked away.

In those times the smallest of things, inconceivable things, caused Negros to be harassed or beaten by the police or sheriff's officers. Henry Chinn, Jr., a CORE task force worker, was arrested for speeding and driving without a driver's license.

"John Chance, a plainclothes detective, questioned me about my involvement in Civil Rights activities," Chinn said, *"and they wanted to know the location of my father. I was then beaten, kicked in the head and stomach with the officers' fists and nightsticks, and then arrested."*

Shortly after that all the CORE team -- Merritt, Watts, Hewitt, Chinn, Collier, and Jewett -- who were in the county jail were moved to the Jackson city jails. Why they were moved is unknown. It might only have been a strategy to break the spirit of the Negros. However, concerned as to why the police knew so much about their movement other than a planted informant in the group, found later that their radio frequencies 8 and 16 was tapped.

In the meantime, Constable Hervey Evans attacked two Negro teens after leaving a voter registration meeting at the Mount Zion Baptist Church. The teenagers were Willie Galloway, Jr., and Arthur Harris. The Constable forced them to stop their truck and then arrested them.

"I was taken behind the city jail," Willie Galloway said, *"and hit in the head and stomach by the police. I was then questions about my father. The constable told me, 'We know that your father had tried to register to vote days ago. It will be good for you that I don't see you at any more meetings, and tell your father, the carpenter, that if he goes to work tomorrow, the men he works*

for will have a mortician there to cart him of the property. You better not tell a person what has happened. If you do, you better just catch the next train to St. Louis.'"

At the same time, Arthur Harris was inside the police station being interrogated about what went on at the meeting. The police wanted to know who the speakers were and what was said at the meeting.

"I was hit multiple times in the head with a rubber siphon hose," Harris said, *"and a nightstick was broken over my head. They also cut lumps of my hair from, my head with a razor. Then they fired at me with a loaded pistol and told me, 'You better not tell a person what happened, or we will put weight around your neck and drop you in the river. If you do come back to Canton, you better be gone by 9:00 p.m..."*

These incidents energized the Negros in Canton to fight more determinedly to achieve their equal rights under the Constitution of the United States than at other times. However, the new Sheriff, Jack Cauthan of Madison County appealed to the people that he had information that certain people, groups, and organization are attempting to cause unrest and friction among the Negros to intimidate the citizens." Further, *"These acts are originated, created, and perpetrated by people other than our own, and the parties active locally are members of a very small minority of Negros,"* said the Sheriff. *"I have coextensive jurisdiction in the cities, and town in our county, I openly state that I will, as chief law enforcement officer in this county enforce the laws to the best of my ability and will suppress any conspiracies designed to create unrest against Madison County." "I will work with any and all law enforcement agencies and governing bodies to maintain peace and dignity of our citizens and community, I will afford all protection of all laws for our citizens."*

Resuming the efforts to curtail Negro activities against the merchants, Mayor Matthew emphasized, *"Each citizen of this city has the absolute and inalienable right to purchase goods and merchandise at any retail store he so desires, regardless of any representations to the contrary made by agitators and other malcontents whose sole purpose is to disrupt the peaceful and harmonious conditions which now prevail in our City."*

Nevertheless, their actions did nothing to stop the boycott and voter registrations in Madison County.

A new month has arrived, February and the U. S. Justice Department was still hearing arguments about the harsh treatment of the Negros in Madison County. As the Negros complained, Sherriff Cauthan reportedly said, *"I enforce the law equally for both races."* The prosecutor thinking that the case was about to take a turn for the worse because the chief witness, Burke Marshall, was sick and could not come to court, the Judge allowed him to read his statement. *"There is not an acceptable federal solution to this law enforcement problem, and we do not have federal police force empowered or equipped to provide protection to or maintain law and order on a generalized basis. As well, I do not believe that the situation, deplorable as it may be in many parts, warrant the departure from the historic pattern of limited federal power that would be implied the creation a federal force having as its purpose the maintenance of internal law and order."* However, later the next day, Burke Marshall resigned because he felt that the Justice Department was not doing enough to protect Negros against excesses' force by the local law enforcement officers.

Nonetheless, the Negros' complaints kept coming. One person, Reverend James McGee of the Madison County movement said, *"I had been threatened and followed by white persons after my involvement in the Negro voter registration. Much of the violence in the areas has been done with the knowledge of law enforcement officers of Madison County."* George Washington, Sr., a Negro grocer who owns the building used as Canton's Freedom House said as he took the stand, *"I was arrested and struck by city policemen when I complained to them about the bombing of property that I rent to the COFO group to use as their headquarter. Also, Dan Thompson, Chief of Police telephoned me and told me he was sorry it happened, and it would not happen again."* Moreover, my mother Susie Mae Brown explained how she was approached by the City Jailer when she tried to bring clothes to her daughter. Mom replied, *"My child Barbara Jean Brown was arrested on May 29 during the second Freedom Day event. I drove to the city jail to bring her some changing clothes. The jailer told me to get my damn ass out of his jail and not to be caught on his property again, or he would lock me up".* She left still clutching her child's clothes. Even though the testimonies' from the Negros continue, there were no acceptable resolution to the problem.

Now, the state leaders knew that things were about to change in consequence of passing the Civil Rights Bill. There were several statements by the White residents of failure, cynicism, objection, and buoyancy. In this case, Cooper, a white man from Yazoo said, *"Mississippians must realize that we have lost the battle, and the 1964 civil rights Act is the law of the land. The habits of yesteryears must be cast aside, and Mississippi must not dwell in the past years, but take the time to change."* While another saw signs of hopefulness in this country but think that those who come here seeking trouble can still find it. As well as, those who goes to a place trying to get in the jailhouse can still find ways to get there. Likewise, the chamber of commerce representative thought the state had shown significant improvement over the years in its intention of complying with the Civil Rights Act. Nonetheless, believed that businesses must work *"With the mainstream America with the expectation of the mainstream working with them."* As well, E. Palmer, a Natchez businessmen held, *"The racial violence in the state cost the state's industry because the manufacturers that were planning to locate here have dropped those ideas. We need to change because nothing is gained by anyone living in the past."* Concerned over the implication of what the outcome of the violence had caused the state, in like manner, Reverend Davis of Jackson articulated, *"Tyranny must go away in the state. It must be clear that anarchy, intolerance, demagoguery, and violence shall not be allowed to prevail in our state."* Moreover, Reverend Allen a Jackson minister troubled about the effectiveness of communication moving forward responded, *"The key word is communication. This concept is missing. We make no claims of great accomplishment, but there had been a considerable concern."* And yet, Rabbi Nussbaum conferring with a higher authority understood, *"Until the clergy will go from preaching in the pulpit to implementing in the pews, we will never accomplish more than slow growth."* While Governor Paul Johnson; on the other hand, maintained the rest of the nation should, *"Get off our back and on our side as the state tries to solve its racial problems."* Finally, after weeks of testimonies, the hearing concluded. Though, Commissioner Hannah acknowledged, *"Some white persons in "far too many countries are seemingly still bent on denying the vote to Negro citizens by the application of discriminatory standards, intimidation, and violence. I hope the thoughtful, and conscientious white leaders of this state will take every step to guarantee the free exercise throughout Mississippi of this fundamental citizenship right. The commission is heartened by the signs of developing consensus among the many responsible white Mississippians who believed that it is poor economics, poor law, and poor morality to encourage or permit racial violence and injustice to continue. Because their physical security is rudimentary to all other rights and the Commission is appalled to find that there are many citizens in some Mississippi communities who fear for their lives."* President Lyndon Johnson entreating the inflexible mindset of most Americans on the subject of the Congressional Civil Rights Act wrote, *"New light is shed on the civil rights movement, and leaders now realized it is time that we must change, or be destroyed by change."*

Although, the Negros of Madison County welcome the passing of the 1964 Civil Rights Act; yet, the 1965 Voting Rights Act was still being ignored. Moore, with the U.S. Justice Department, was already in town dealing with the pending justice case against Foote Campbell when he received a knock of his motel door at the Bill Will Motel. When Moore answered; many local ministers introduced themselves and told him why they wanted to speak with him. Moore warmly greeted the men and let them in.

After the ministers had discussed their concerns, Moore went to Campbell's office, but the office was closed. Given that this was a week-day viewed uncommon to Moore. As soon as the Sheriff learned that Moore was at the Circuit Clerk's office, he contacted Foote Campbell and instructed him to open his office.

There were FBI agents in town and members of the National Council of Churches, Student Non-Violent Coordinating Committee and the lo-cal branch of the NAACP all waiting to see what Foote Campbell would do. When he opened the courthouse doors on the west side of the build-ing, twenty-five Negros entered the building, but only three at a time were allowed to take the registration exam. By 3:00 p.m., there were six-ty-six more Negros in line waiting their turn to take the test. Campbell still would not allow any more than three people in at a time. Moore then entered the Circuit Clerk's office and posted a legal notice of the 1965 Voting Rights Act that read, *"It is a crime to intimidate, threaten or coerce, or attempt to intimidate any person performing his duties under the Voting Rights Act of 1965."*

The courageous Annie Devine diligently worked to get as many Negros registered to vote in the upcoming October election as possible. She was a pivotal force in the voter registration movement in Canton that led to more than 100 Negros registered voters.

In the meantime, as a large number of Negros were inside the office of the registrar's, a large group of Negro students was on the outside picketing Fred's Dollar and Iupe Fair Department Stores. The picketers held signs telling people not to trade with either establishment because the owners discriminated against Negros. As the Negros marched in front of the two stores, many young white men threw eggs, bottles, rocks, sticks and spikes at them. The police came, but when the mob of young whites ran past the police, not one of them was arrested.

Immediately after this incident, Martin Luther King, Jr., and the SNCC director Stokely Carmichael held a tent meeting at the Nichols Middle Negro School football field. Upset by what they saw, the man reminded the crowd that more could be achieved without violence than could be with violence.

As Martin was speaking, Sheriff's deputies and police officers walked onto the football field and pulled down the tents while the meeting was still in progress. One deputy informed King and Carmichael that they were told not to pitch the *"dam"* tents on school property. The crowd became agitated, and the officers sprayed tear gas into their faces while they physically forced them to leave the meeting place. Many Negros were injured from the brutality of the police and deputies pushing and dragging them off the property.

The next day the NAACP split off into groups. One group went to Philadelphia in cars while Martin Luther King, Jr. flew there in a helicopter. A second group of Negros stayed and marched from Canton to Tougaloo. A third group made up of a small number of Negros and whites marched from the Holy Child Jesus Catholic Church to the courthouse on Peace Street. Many city officials stopped them at the south gate.

"What's your business here?" the marchers were asked.

"To register to vote," their leader said.

They were not let in, and the crowd began screaming and shouting.

"We want power. When do we want it? Now! Black Power! Black Power!"

Many of the demonstrators sat down in the middle of Peace Street and blocked traffic for hours. Others drove up and down the main street and around the city on the tops of automobile hoods shouting, *"Power now!"*

CHAPTER EIGHT

A Cry for Mercy

At this time, the KKK had gathered and were standing waving their flags and shouting back, *"Niggers have no power now and no power tomorrow."*

There were Negro students picketing Fred's Dollar Store that day, too. Barbara Jean was with them and at one point; she snatched the Citizens' Council sticker off the store's front door.

"Nigger bitch, I'll kick your ass," The store manager, Billy, yelled at her as he ran out of the store.

"Kick my ass? Kiss my ass," Barbara Jean shouted right back at him.

"You nigger bitch, you will not live to see your next birthday," Billy yelled back at her.

The words continued back and forth between them, louder and louder until Eddie Mixon pulled Barbara Jean away from the store and made her go home.

On Saturday, December 24, a cold night just before that Christmas, Barbara Jean was getting ready to celebrate her eighteenth birthday with friends. As usual, she wore her hair pinned up with her favorite hair bows. She was a young, energized woman who only wanted to enjoy the night dancing and to have a good time. She did not realize that this was her last night of partying.

She connected with friends Tessie and Mary and the three of them went to the local hot spot, Jimmy Sims Café on West Peace Street in the Negro section of town. As soon as they arrived at the nightspot, Jessie Lee Pate, a heavy, dark complexioned young man in his twenties, told Barbara Jean to leave with him.

"I did not think there was anything to it because Jessie was a friend of ours," Tessie later said, *"at least not until I saw the knife. Barbara Jean was forced to leave with him. Jessie held the knife to Barbara Jean's back and forced her to leave. We waited and waited for her to come back, but she never did. After a while, we left the café and went to Barbara Jean's home."*

In the first morning hours of Christmas day, I heard knocking on the door. It had woken mother and me. My mother usually wouldn't answer the door that late, but this knocking sounded as if it was at the end of someone's tether. I felt a sinking feeling in my stomach as mother blundered in the dark to the door.

"Who is it?" mother asked.

The voice on the other side of the door answered. It was Tessie. I could hear her blubbing trying to hold back the tears. Mother opened the door to let Tessie and Mary in. They were both crying, hysterically.

"Is Barbara Jean home?" Tessie asked.

"No, she left with y'all," mother replied.

"Yes, ma, but she left the café with Jessie," Tessie said. *"We thought that she may have come home."*

Mother jaw dropped when she heard the name Jessie. He was already known as the "bad" boy from Indianapolis. Deep motherly instinct told her that something was wrong, and she became beside yourself and ran off into the cold December night looking for her child, but to no avail. When she came home, she sat up the rest of the night praying that her child would be all right.

"Lord, please bring my child home, Lord," she kept repeating.

On that cold Christmas morning, while people were opening, Christmas gifts and drinking eggnog, my sister was still missing.

Later that afternoon, many neighborhood children were out riding their new bikes when they saw a body lying in a ditch near the railway track. The body was Barbara Jean's, dead at the age of seventeen, one day before her birthday. Her body had been beaten, cut into pieces, and mutilated beyond recognition.

The FBI, the sheriff, and the county coroners were informed. The local coroner's jury, summoned afterward by coroner Breeland, ruled that the death was due to injuries perpetrated by the hand of a person or persons unknown. The pathologist's jury ordered a pathologist test to be performed on the body, as well.

That Christmas day instead of singing Christmas carols, I went with mother to the crime scene. When we arrived, I watched dreadfulness the devastated and disconcerted look on mother's face as she beheld at the unpardonable horror of her child's disfigured body.

"Lord, have mercy on me," she cried out. *"Lord have mercy, my child is gone."*

Words cannot begin to describe the sight of my sister's bloody body lying there maimed at the hand of some monster. I wondered if she had been laying there all night in the frigid winter temperature screaming for help, but help never arrived. I wondered how it was that no one stopped to hear the cries in the night of a young girl cry for help. Maybe she never had time to cry out. Maybe there the good LORD silently like a ghost called her home that night. I hope He did.

Looking at my sister's body that night was a horrendous and gruesome sight that has never left my mind. Nobody should die in that manner. When mother finally pulled herself together to identify her daughter's body, she was only able to recognize her child by the bows that she wore in her hair that night before leaving home to celebrate her eighteen birthday. The body was too disfigured to be identified by any other means.

The FBI interviewed many people living near the railroad tracks, but they all stated that they did not hear or see anything. How difficult could it have been not to hear a cry in the peaceful night? Officials did find a cap that was left at the crime scene, and they believed it must have belonged to the person who committed the murder.

The investigators interviewed Tessie and Mary, who were with her the night she died, and they told the investigators that they saw Jessie Lee Pate wearing a cap that looked like the cap they had found. Based on their testimony, Jessie Lee Pate was charged for murder. He was arrested at the home of his relative, six miles west of Canton in the Tin Top community that Christmas night. When the constables arrived, Jessie Lee Pate was still in bed, still dressed in the clothes he had presumably worn at the time of the murder.

Judge Lee Hendricks, at the preliminary hearing on December 30th, ordered a psychiatric evaluation at the state mental institution at Whitfield, where he is committed Jessie into custody until his trial date, September 1966.

In the meantime, mother had prepared to bury her daughter at the Stokes Chapel Missionary Baptist Church on Stokes Road in Flora, Mississippi. All of Barbara Jean's friends and schoolmates, many members of the NAACP, some out-of-town guests, and relatives gathered to mourn and give their last respects to a young woman cut down even before the prime of her life. However, I believed as did others that Barbara Jean's death was a warning to the Negros that if they continue to boycott and integrate their schools and businesses the same thing would happen to them. I believe, too, that the people heeded the warning because things slowed down, but did not stopped.

On September 1966, Judge Lee Hendricks sentenced Jessie Lee Pate to fifteen years in prison.

Researching this book took me back to a familiar place, filled with unapproachable pain. Time after time, I tried to forget. Can I ever forget? No.

The death of my sister has always haunted me. It was an abysmal time in my life and an extreme setback to our family. I always believed that more than one person caused Barbara Jean's death. Barbara Jean's size and ability to fight back and protect herself made it impossible that only one person could overtake her in that manner.

After graduating from Canton High School in 1972, I moved away. However, the vision of my sister's mutilated body continued to haunt me. Against all my emotions, I still wanted to find out what really happened to her because, in my mind, I felt that there was someone who knew what had happened.

Later, after I had returned to Canton, I found people who had lived near the murder scene. They told me that they were too afraid to speak out then but they did hear Barbara Jean's cry. When they had looked out their windows, they saw three men beating somebody. One of the men was black, and the other two were white. They said that the two white men were beating the person and a black man looked as if he was cutting and stamping the person.

They said that if they had only known that it was Ms. Brown's daughter, they would have tried to help.

Tessie, who had met Barbara Jean during the civil rights movement, told me, *"Barbara Jean snatched the Citizens' Council sticker off Fred's*

Dollar Store's door, a manager with curly red hair ran out the store and shook his finger in her face and had told her she wouldn't live to see her next birthday."

"Barbara Jean said to him, 'Kiss my ass." Tessie told me. *"That girl was not afraid of anything. Rumors were that it was this redheaded man who had paid Jessie Pate to kill Barbara Jean. That theory is the most plausible. I could not understand why Jessie would do that. He was her friend. How could he do that? If we had gone with her that night, we would have died too."*

Bob, a family friend, told me another part of the story. He said that he had seen Jessie, who was sometimes known as Dick, on Friday, December 23.

"I am leaving in the morning," Jessie had said to Bob, *"and catching a ride with Willie back to Indianapolis."*

About 1:00 p.m. on Saturday, December 24, 1965, Bob said that he saw Jessie walking up the road with those boots he had on, supposedly the same ones that stumped Barbara Jean to death. Bob said to himself, *"Jessie didn't leave with Willie."*

Bob found out later that Willie had told Jessie that he could not ride back with them because the back seats only fit two people comfortably, and the small middle bumper seat would make it too uncomfortable for him to ride all the way back to Indianapolis with Willie.

Bob told me that Jessie had said to him on that Saturday, *"I will do anything for some money."* Bob last saw him walking off by himself.

That Saturday night, December 24th, Bob saw Jessie sitting alone at Johnny Sims Cafe. When Bob and his friends were leaving the café, Bob saw Johnny Gray, a friend of Jessie's, coming into the café and walking over to Dick's table. Bob and his friends went their separate ways, not thinking anything was about to happen.

On Sunday, Christmas day, Bob told me that people came through the neighborhood and said that Barbara Jean was dead and that Jessie was the one who had killed her. When Bob ran into Johnny Gray, the person he'd seen with Jessie the night before, Johnny told Bob, *"I did not do it. I did not kill Bennie's sister. Jessie and Riddle was with her."*

Bob also told me that Jessie was in bed with those bloody boots on the night the police arrested him; the same boots used to stump Barbara Jean.

"Why are you in bed?" the police had asked him.

"I didn't do nothing," he replied. *"I didn't do nothing."*

Nevertheless, the police found his bloody clothes under the mattress.

"That nigger was crazy," Bob said to me.

Much later, after Jessie had served his time, he went to work at the dairy factory just west of Canton. He took his boss' truck one day and crashed it. The truck went up in a blaze of flames and Jessie was burned over ninety percent of his body. He was taken to the Greenwood burn center, and the doctors needed to amputate his legs, but he would not let them because he wanted to see Susie, and he did not want to die before seeing her.

The theory has it that white folks paid Jessie to kill Barbara Jean because she was picketing Fred's Dollar Store. The store belonged to Charles Riddell and his son, Tom.

My mother and I ran into Jessie one day after he had gotten out of prison. We were at the Exxon Station on Highway 22 getting gasoline when he came over to my mother's car and told her he wanted to talk with her. I refused to let my mother talk with him. My mother looked as if she ached to communicate with him, as he asserted that he had something to tell her about her daughter, but I drove off.

Seeing him brought back so much pain to me from the memory of seeing my sister's body lying mutilated in the ditch that night. It was too much to suppress.

"May he rest in hell," was all I could say to my mother as we drove off.

Later, we heard about Jessie's traffic accident as soon as it had happened. As he lay dying in the Greenwood burn center, he requested to see my mother. This time I did not challenge the request. Mother went to the hospital.

When she returned from seeing him, I asked what had happened.

"Jessie told me that he killed Barbara Jean, but not alone," she said. *"But he died before telling me who the other men were that helped him kill her."*

Susie had never been the same after Barbara Jean's murder, though she tried her best to be happy. The pain of losing her child in that manner always showed on her face. I believe the only good thing about it all was the great support that my mother had from friends like Mamie Sojourner, Mamie Small, Molly and Mae Lena Jackson, Ida Bennett, Annie Gross, Lou Emma Anthony, Lou Emma Jackson, Julia Small, Vietter Davis, Louise Jackson, and so many more. Sadly, Susie died in 2009 before knowing the whole truth behind her child's murder.

Those names have never been revealed, and all the key players are long gone.

However, "For the eyes of the LORD is over the righteous, and his ears are open unto their prayers: but the face of the Lord is against them that do evil" (1 Peter 3:12).